READING WILLIAM BLAKE

William Blake (1757–1827) is one of the most original and influential figures of the Romantic Age, known for his work as an artist, poet and printmaker. Grounding his ideas both in close reading and in the latest scholarship, Saree Makdisi offers an exciting and imaginative approach to reading Blake. By exploring some of the most important themes in Blake's work and connecting them to particular plates from *Songs of Innocence and of Experience*, Makdisi highlights Blake's creative power and the important interplay between images and words. There is a consistent emphasis on the relationship between the material nature of Blake's illuminated books, including the method he used to produce them, and the interpretive readings of the texts themselves. Makdisi argues that the material and formal openness of Blake's work can be seen as the very basis for learning to read in the spirit of Blake.

SAREE MAKDISI is Professor of English and Comparative Literature at the University of California, Los Angeles. He is the author of *Making England Western* (2014), *Palestine Inside Out: An Everyday Occupation* (2010), *William Blake and the Impossible History of the 1790s* (2003), and *Romantic Imperialism* (Cambridge, 1998).

READING WILLIAM BLAKE

SAREE MAKDISI

CAMBRIDGE
UNIVERSITY PRESS

CAMBRIDGE
UNIVERSITY PRESS

University Printing House, Cambridge CB2 8BS, United Kingdom

Cambridge University Press is part of the University of Cambridge.

It furthers the University's mission by disseminating knowledge in the pursuit of education, learning and research at the highest international levels of excellence.

www.cambridge.org
Information on this title: www.cambridge.org/9780521128414

First published 2015
Reprinted 2015

A catalogue record for this publication is available from the British Library

Library of Congress Cataloguing in Publication data
Makdisi, Saree.
Reading William Blake / Saree Makdisi.
pages cm
Includes bibliographical references and index.
ISBN 978-0-521-76303-5 (Hardback) – ISBN 978-0-521-12841-4 (Paperback)
1. Blake, William, 1757–1827–Criticism and interpretation.   I. Title.
PR4147.M34 2014
821'.7–dc23
2014039050

ISBN 978-0-521-76303-5 Hardback
ISBN 978-0-521-12841-4 Paperback

For my aunt Grace

Contents

Illustrations

Acknowledgments

This book would not have been possible without the help of many people.

Morris Eaves and Kevin Gilmartin provided constructive criticism of the original version of what turned into the present book. My mother, Jean Said Makdisi, read through the chapters of the final version as I wrote them and provided reader-response criticism of the best variety. Robert Essick kindly read through the final manuscript and provided thoughtful and detailed criticisms as well as a very generous note of approval. Blair Hoxby provided me with some suggestions for sharpening my account of the English Revolution and related matters. I am greatly indebted to them all, though, needless to say, any remaining flaws are my own responsibility.

I have learned a great deal about Blake and the process of printing from copper plates from hours spent printing from the rolling press at Morley College in London with Michael Phillips, to whom I am also indebted.

The study of Blake's work involves working with images and reproducing them in print. I am grateful to Angela Roche and Chris Sutherns at the British Museum, Scott Wilcox and Melissa Fournier at the Yale Center for British Art, Emma Darbyshire at the Fitzwilliam Museum, and Joe Fletcher at the Blake Archive for helping me acquire the images from their respective collections. And I owe a big thanks to Joe Viscomi for all of his help and guidance in navigating the world of images and rights, and for his many patient answers to my questions about images.

I am especially grateful to the Blake Archive for making the study of the visual side of Blake so much more possible, and to the Library of Congress and the Yale Center for British Art for their generous open access policy, which is a model that ought to inspire other collections.

Finally, I'd like to thank Anna Bond and Linda Bree at Cambridge University Press, especially Linda for proposing the project to me, and for her patience over the years as it gradually took shape.

And, as always, I must acknowledge Christina, Samir, and Maissa for putting up with me during the long moments of distraction sometimes demanded by this book.

This book is dedicated to my Aunt Grace, who embodies the spirit of kindness, generosity, commitment, and joy that we see everywhere in Blake.

Introduction

I'm not sure that William Blake would have liked the idea of this book. He certainly thought his work needed no explanatory introduction. "You say that I want somebody to Elucidate my Ideas," he once wrote to a reader who complained to him that his work was too difficult to understand. "But I am happy to find a Great Majority of Fellow Mortals who can Elucidate My Visions & Particularly they have been Elucidated by Children who have taken a greater delight in contemplating my Pictures than I even hoped."[1] No matter how accessible Blake thought his work was, however, its reputation for difficulty has been sustained rather than reduced by the plethora of guidebooks and handbooks intended to help readers approach what he called his illuminated books. There are now many guides and companions to Blake (not to mention countless essays or articles or book chapters devoted to readings and explications of each one of the illuminated books). Many, going back all the way to S. Foster Damon's 1965 *Blake Dictionary*, have been written with the primary intention of making Blake more accessible by helping readers decipher or decode particular texts.

And yet there remains a great deal of truth to Blake's assertion that his works need no elucidation. It's not just that the more layers of interpretation we add to our approach to any one of Blake's texts, the more difficult that approach ends up being, but also that if we read Blake through all those layers we run the risk of losing much of what is most exciting and original about his work – we end up reading the layers, as it were, rather than gaining access to the work itself. When I teach Blake to undergraduate students, I urge them to dispense with the commentaries and notes offered by most editions of his work, and to read the words and images on their own rather than as filtered through the commentaries. I also tell them that every single time I have taught Blake over the past two decades, I have witnessed undergraduate readers in the classroom propose, on their very first approach to Blake, ingenious and exciting interpretations and readings of particular lines or images or words that have never occurred to me and (far more significantly) have never been advanced in the proliferating scholarship on Blake.

That, of course, reinforces Blake's claim about the openness and accessibility of his work. No matter how much we have written about him, there is always more to see, to read, and to discover – and the best such readings and discoveries can come precisely from untrained and uninitiated readers, rather than solely from the body of scholarly experts licensed to talk about Blake. This should not, of course, be taken to diminish the value of the many books on (or guides and companions to) Blake, to which I have made my own previous contributions, I should confess. Nor should it diminish the value of teaching Blake or studying him in a class as opposed to reading him on one's own, since we can always find yet more to discover in these astonishing works when we think them through from a variety of different vantage points, or with particular questions in mind. But it does raise the question of why the world needs yet another guide to reading William Blake.

What I want to offer in the present volume, however, is neither a guide nor a companion, certainly not a guide or companion to specific poems, images, books, or other works by Blake, and absolutely not a decoding manual claiming to provide the definitive reading or explanation of this or that character, name, line, image, or reference in Blake's work. I don't think particular works by Blake should be read through the optic or filter or an interpretive frame or a commentary provided by someone else. Rather than offering such a filter or interpretive frame, what I propose in this book is a set of discussions of some of the most important concepts in Blake's work; concepts that, in our age, have come to acquire very different meanings and implications from what they used to signify in Blake's age. These discussions are not intended to frame or filter particular readings of specific works by Blake but rather simply to open up what I hope will be useful ways of thinking about them. In other words, the discussions I provide here are intended to help you develop your own readings and interpretations of Blake's work rather than imposing mine on you ("thy phantasy has imposed upon me," protests the Angel in one of the Memorable Fancies of *The Marriage of Heaven and Hell;* "& thou oughtest to be ashamed.")[2] I should add right away that the book is devoted specifically to Blake the author and printer of illuminated books (and to some of the major themes running through the latter). There are other Blakes, of course, and Blake the painter of watercolors and temperas, or Blake the intaglio engraver of his own masterpieces (such as his illustrations for the Book of Job) won't receive much attention in what is to follow.

It's useful to discuss Blake's key ideas and to try to locate them in the situation and moment out of which his work emerged because many readings of Blake approach him from the standpoint of the culture (or to be precise the particular strand of the culture) of modernity that was being consolidated in his own time – and hence they fail to recognize Blake's antipathy to that culture and his refusal of many of its core principles. Since he came from the emergent age of individualism, for example, he has often been read as a steadfast individualist, even though individual self-hood as we normally think of that notion is not only not particularly evident as a structuring principle of his work but is repeatedly scorned or condemned by it. Since he can be seen to share various forms of affiliation with the mainstream radicals of his day – including a distaste for the hereditary power of England's traditional political elite – he has long been seen as an advocate of the rights of man in the mold of Tom Paine or the artisan activists of the London Corresponding Society (one of the earliest organizations dedicated to the cause of British democracy). The word "rights" doesn't occur anywhere in the illuminated books, however, whereas "desire," the very bane of London radicalism (which often saw itself as engaged in a war against the unregulated desires of a dissipated and indulgent, "unmanly," or Orientalized aristocracy) is one of the most important principles driving Blake's work. Since the work is replete with many adoring references to Christ, he has long been read in conventional Christian terms, even though "priests" are right next to "kings" in his array of villains, and churches collapsed into palaces and prisons. And his many references to England have long been taken to justify views of him as a jingoistic nationalist, even though his work makes it clear that he sees the lineaments of God in "every man from every clime," and not only in Englishmen.

Trying to force Blake to fit the interpretive grid of the dominant form of modernity that structures our present-day world doesn't work because he was at odds with so many of its ideas and values. In an age of individualism, he articulated a view of our being that insisted that each of us is tied in with and inseparable from others, and that we share a common unity in God. In an age of war and commerce, he insisted on the values of love and the imagination. At the very peak of the industrial revolution, he invented a method of printing that stood the logic of industrial production on its head, using its technologies to slowly and laboriously produce a stream of handcrafted artworks that bore no relation whatsoever to the endless flood of cheap mass-produced commodities that was already beginning to wash over England and the rest of the world. And in an age when the British empire was beginning to accumulate more and more territory and to dominate the lives of millions of people around the world, Blake refused the idea that one people could claim superiority over another, and he steadfastly rejected the notions of war, occupation, massacre, and ethnic cleansing that have been the hallmarks of empire in the modern age.

If all this makes Blake sound as though he was out of synch with his own time, there is certainly truth in that. And yet the other way of thinking that he was out of synch with his own time is to suggest that he also saw the potential carried within modernity for creating a very different kind of world, more closely integrated and networked, and yet also fairer, motivated by principles of love and sharing rather than aggressive, acquisitive selfishness. Strangely enough, this makes Blake all the more valuable for us not only as a figure to be more thoroughly grounded and located in his time, but also as an observer and a critic of our own, since it was in his day that our age was violently given birth. In observing our age from an odd angle, he helps us better understand it.

Both his profession and his location may have helped him in this. As I mentioned briefly and return to discuss at greater length in the chapters to follow, his status as a professional engraver – but one who used the printing technology of copperplate engraving to stand its reproductive commercial logic on its head – gave him a uniquely privileged standpoint from which to think through and develop a critique of an industrial culture that was based precisely on the same logic of blind repetition and unimaginative copying, essential to commercial engraving, that Blake set out to subvert and contest. And his status as a Londoner gave him an unobstructed view of the emergence and development of a global system of empire and exploitation from its very center.

Indeed, London in Blake's time was altered beyond recognition by the same processes of empire and commercial and industrial growth that would go on to transform the rest of the world. In his own lifetime he would have seen his native Soho be transformed from a heterogeneous and unevenly cosmopolitan district at what had been the edge of the urban built-up area to one caught on the wrong side of the virtual wall between the "respectable" and the "unrespectable" that was developed in John Nash's Regent Street project. Regent Street, London's first modern urban renewal project, was designed to introduce speed and movement into densely packed urban neighborhoods. In so doing, it separated those parts of the metropolis where freedom of circulation and of communication were privileged from those other parts where everything seemed to grind to a halt in disorderly degradation. The project was in that sense, as Nash himself put it, designed to effect "a boundary and complete separation between the inhabitants of the first classes of society, and those of the inferior classes."[3] The very same lines of distinction and axes of superiority and inferiority, development and underdevelopment, civilization and barbarism, Occidentalism and Orientalism, that helped to define the world-space of empire were also in play and actively imposed on London itself. Not only would Blake have rubbed shoulders with people from every corner of the planet, but his frequent walks between Soho and the City, where he worked with publishers including the great Joseph Johnson, would have taken him right through the area of Seven Dials and St. Giles's, whose inhabitants came to be seen from the standpoint of the prosperous and respectable as culturally, civilizationally, and racially indistinguishable from those of India or Africa or Arabia: a third-world Orient right in the middle of Westernizing London.[4] Toward the end of such a walk, or as he would have prepared to turn right to cross Blackfriars Bridge over to Lambeth (where he moved in the 1790s), Blake would have seen the very embodiments of state and religious power so frequently condemned in his work. At the junction of Fleet Street and Ludgate Hill across what had been the Fleet Market, for example – the crossroads linking the publishing world around St. Paul's Churchyard, where Joseph Johnson's shop was, with Blake's residences at one time or another in Soho and Lambeth – he would have taken in, in all but a single glance, the commercial charters "near where the charter'd Thames does flow," the Fleet Prison, the notorious Bridewell workhouse, the shadow of Newgate Prison just a little farther along and, rising above it all, the great dome of St. Paul's. That conjuncture – commerce, state, and religious power all in a single glance – gives new meaning to the cries and groans we hear in "London" in *Songs of Experience*.

Each of the following short chapters offers a brief discussion of what I see as the most important concepts animating Blake's illuminated books, from joy and desire to power and making. To ground the discussion, I have focused each chapter on a reading of one of the *Songs of Innocence and of Experience*, the work that is generally regarded as the "gateway drug" to the world of Blake's illuminated books since it is both accessible and widely available – and is also by far the most likely text with which any student of Blake will begin. The readings and arguments are offered with the aim of opening up pathways and avenues into Blake's work and his ideas. It will quickly be evident that I think Blake's work need not be – and really cannot be – read systematically, since by its very nature it offers an open network through which we can trace our own interpretive paths. I hope these chapters will be read in the same way as you find and pick up what is useful and what gives you something to think with or of or about and leave behind that which does not. They are offered in the hope that you will quickly develop your own way to read in the spirit of Blake.

CHAPTER I

Image

Two major and obvious features distinguish Blake's work from that of most other poets. The first is that for the most part it consists of both words and pictures; the second is that it exists as a heterogeneous collection of books manually produced by Blake himself. These features will mark the point of departure for our approach to Blake.

There is a catch, however – and it's the kind of catch that makes reading Blake so frustrating for some people, and so immensely exciting and rewarding for the rest of us. Actually, there are two catches.

The first catch is that neither words nor pictures in Blake's work function in what we might (even provisionally) think of as the usual way. For example, the pictures don't simply illustrate the words in the way that they often seem to in books containing pictures – and quite often they seem to have nothing to do with the words at all. Rather than thinking of the pictures as secondary, or as mere supplements to the words, then, it's more helpful to think of Blake's works as being two quasi-independent texts: a verbal one (the words) and a visual one (the images). Even this approach, though, is complicated as sometimes the images and the words in Blake's texts lose their respective distinctiveness and seem to merge into one another. Look at all those letters, on the title page of *Songs of Innocence and of Experience* among other places, where letters sprout tendrils and branches and take on other pictorial characteristics, making it difficult or impossible to establish a clean differentiation between words and pictures. It's most helpful, then, to think of Blake's works as constituted by and existing in the charged and ever-changing relationship between the restlessly mutating verbal and visual components of which it is composed, and even to think of the text as somehow suspended – activated, charged, turned on – in the gap between those components: a gap that every reader traces in a different way with every encounter with the work.

The second catch has to do with the material nature of Blake's books and the printing method he used to produce them. It is vital to bear in mind when reading them that they are not books in conventional letter-press format, but rather a series of bound sets of etched prints. The experience of reading them thus straddles the line between turning the pages of a conventional book and looking at a series of individual prints or paintings. Even when they compose parts of a story or a series of stories, Blake's works were, necessarily, produced plate by plate. This allowed him to think of the sub-components constituting his works as building blocks from which the larger works could be composed.

And this in turn allowed Blake to think of how each sub-component operates semi-autonomously or in relation to other neighboring sub-components – and hence to think of his larger works as a series of arrangements or re-arrangements of these same sub-components that could be variously modified, altered, shuffled, and replaced, with each such variation changing the larger structures of which they form parts, though – and this is the point – without losing their characteristic coherence. We might say, borrowing from the principles of physics, that Blake's books have high entropy: there are many ways that each book's constituent elements can be arranged and re-arranged without subverting the overall structure of the book whereas we might say that another kind of book, like a novel, has low entropy, in that even a minor re-arrangement of its constituent elements would cause the overall structure to collapse in disorder.[1] Or, to turn to the language of philosophy rather than physics, we might say that Blake would have thought of his works as bodies constituted according to the philosophical principle of *immanence*: as wholes that exist only – and in an ever-changing way – in the parts composing them, rather than as constant, unchanging, *transcendent* forces endowed with an existence independent of the parts of which they are composed. (We will see in later chapters that this principle of immanence, expressed in such a profound material way in the form and function of Blake's books, was also central to his political and religious thought.)

Thus Blake's relationship to his works bears little relationship to a modern author's usual relationship to his or her text, given that authors have come to be alienated from the material process of production that connects their texts to the world, and, in general, depending on how you look at it, are either freed from the burden of having to think – or are deprived of the exciting possibilities enabled by thinking – about their works as material bits and pieces that have to somehow fit together. (In writing this book, for example, I am thinking of the overall text, not of this page or the next one as discrete units that might perhaps be aligned in a range of other – possibly more interesting – relationships, changing from one copy to another of *Reading William Blake*: a prospect that I suspect neither the typesetter nor Cambridge University Press would find particularly enticing.)

Having etched the words and images constituting what we might think of as the skeleton of each page on copper plates, Blake printed them, sometimes in different colored inks, and then in many copies fleshed out each print with watercolors and various other forms of detailing. The outcome of this idiosyncratic method of printing was, far from a stream of identical copies of a single original, an endlessly playful series of variations on a theme – in fact, a cluster of related themes spreading across and tying together Blake's different books. As a result, not only are no two copies of any of Blake's prints (of individual plates of *Songs of Innocence*, for example) identical to one another but neither are any two copies of any one book (*Songs of Innocence*, for example).

Apart from all the differences emerging from the printing process itself, which enabled a wide and ever-changing range of color palettes, finishes, details, tones, and textures, there are many variations of sequences and arrangements of the plates among the various copies of *Songs of Innocence and of Experience*. Some plates are missing from certain copies of *Songs*, for instance; or they appear in one sequence in certain copies and in a different sequence in others; or they are included with *Innocence* in certain copies and with *Experience* in others. In some copies, the plates are printed recto and verso (front and back of a leaf of paper), so that in the finished book they sit face to face; in others, they are only printed recto, yielding a very different reading experience, not to mention a very different interpretive framework.

Now, at first glance – if we think about Blake's books in material terms rather than as free-floating poems – these catches might seem to present an almost impenetrable set of obstacles to the successful explication of the work. How can one meaningfully talk about a book when it exists not as one stable object but as an ever-shifting pattern of sights and colors, more akin to a sound-and-light performance than a book in the ordinary – or, rather, the modern – sense? Try to imagine discussing the work of Charles Dickens, for example, if every single copy of *Oliver Twist* had a different sequence of chapters, if in certain copies chapters 12 and 13 were missing, while other copies had two chapter 15s, others had chapters 11 through 14 occurring right between chapters 2 and 3, still others offered a range of a dozen different endings – and yet others dispensed with the bother of an ending at all. Reading, let alone interpreting and discussing, such a novel, as such, would seem an absurd task.

However, what would prove disabling in the case of a novel (which can usefully be thought of in this context as a modern, industrial, mass-produced object, with low entropy, in which order, consistency, and reproducibility are as integral as they are in the production of dishwashers or automobiles) turns out to be profoundly *enabling* in the case of Blake's high-entropy works, which were, far from being mass produced, the products of a slow, inefficient, labor-intensive, archaic, and wonderfully anachronistic method of production. (Part of the point of Blake's work, however – and we will revisit this point at greater length in later chapters – is to push us to think about the extent to which we too often overestimate the normalizing stability of more conventional forms of textuality, including novels: after all, even if you and I are both reading identical copies of the Penguin edition of *Oliver Twist*, my experience of the novel is going to be different from yours; Blake's works literalize that interpretive phenomenon, materially reminding us of the extent to which *all* texts, no matter how solid and authoritative they may seem or claim to be, are actually unstable and open to interpretation).

The key to enjoying Blake's work, then, is embracing – rather than trying to ignore or smother into a kind of norm – what makes it different, and seeing that very difference as offering the point of departure for reading the work in the first place.

What I want to propose now is a way to approach and think through Blake's work that takes its special characteristics into account. And I want to do so in the spirit of Blake himself, not by outlining an abstract set of rules and principles and then finding a text to which they can be applied from the top down by way of example, but rather the other way around: by following the lead of a text and seeing where it allows us to go. And the text I have in mind is the Introduction to *Songs of Innocence* (see Figure 1.1).

Let's begin at the most basic level, simply reading it as a poem – though, as we will see, works by Blake quickly encourage us to move beyond the level of the words. Following the encounter of the speaker with a flying child (don't worry: there are more surprising things in Blake), the five stanzas trace the sequence of the shifting modes of performance requested by the child and offered by the speaker. When he enters the scene, the speaker is "piping songs of pleasant glee." The child asks him to "pipe a song about a Lamb," then to "sing thy songs of happy chear," and, finally, to "sit thee down and write / In a book that all may read." Each time, the

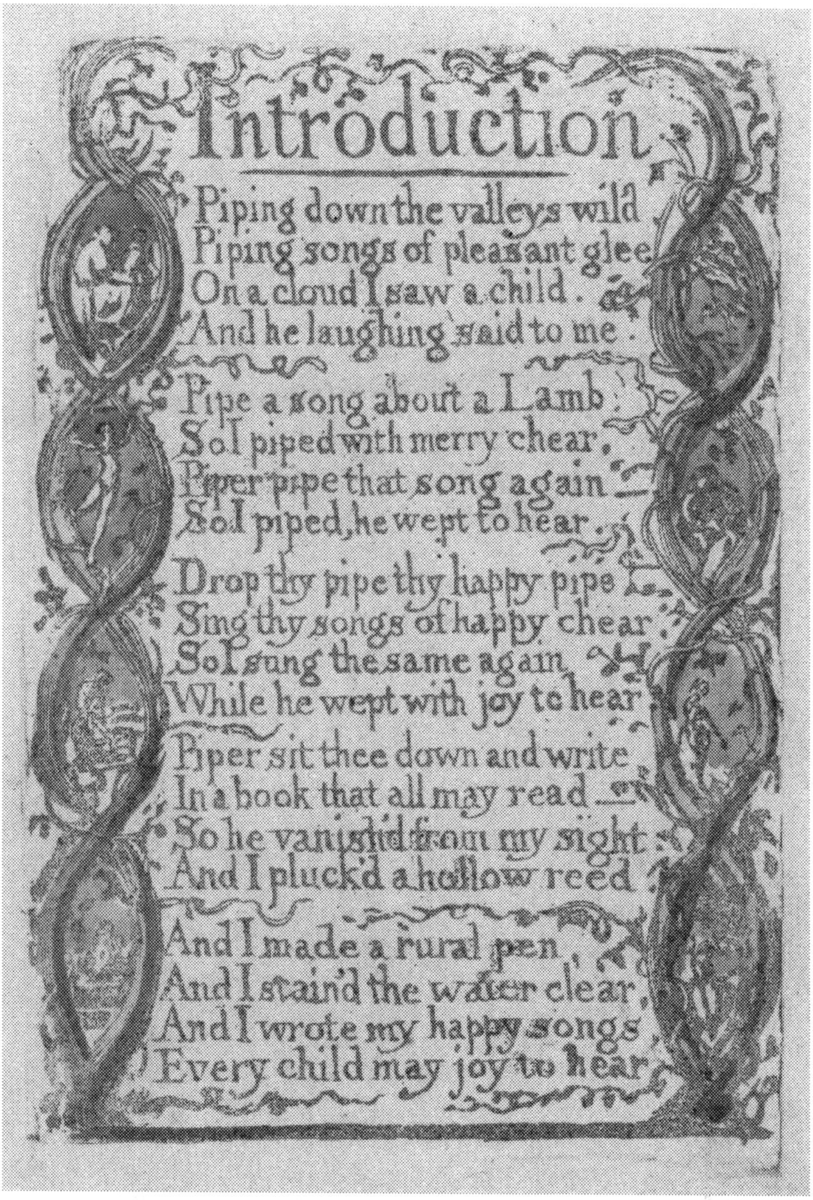

FIGURE 1.1.   "Introduction" from *Songs of Innocence and of Experience*, copy G, plate 3.

speaker responds by taking up the challenge, shifting from playing abstract music ("songs of pleasant glee"), to representational music ("a song about a Lamb"), to singing "the same" (we'll come back to what that might mean), to, finally, writing.

Two points are worth noting right away.

First, the poem traces at once a series of shifts in aesthetic media (musical instrument, human voice, book; piping, singing, writing) and audience responses to those different media. As the media progress, the intensity of the response – and in particular that of the relationship between the performer and the audience – deteriorates, from the initial "I piped, he wept" (where performance and reception are essentially simultaneous), to "I sung the same again / While he wept with joy to hear" (where, with the shift in medium, the relationship of response to performance has been drawn out and somewhat deferred), to, finally, the disappearance of the child and the total deferral of the now unseen, unrecorded audience response to the written book ("I wrote my happy songs, / Every child may joy to hear").

The second point worth noting is that what seems to be a linear account (whether of progress or deterioration or of both) is actually also a circular one, as that last line announces. For when the future and at least potentially universal "every child" encounters the now written book, the encounter takes place not in visual terms but in aural ones all over again: although this is a book "that all may read," the reading is, apparently paradoxically, *heard* rather than simply *seen*. Thus it's no coincidence that the last line, "Every child may joy to *hear*," although it refers to the written book, nevertheless deliberately echoes the earlier references to the reception of the piper's live performance ("he wept to *hear*," "he wept with joy to *hear*"). Having gone in what seemed to be a straight line from sound to writing and hence toward what many take to be the universal, then, we have come full circle back to a particular child hearing. *Plus ça change, plus c'est la même chose*: nowhere does the French expression ("the more something changes, the more it stays the same") ring more true than in Blake, pushing us to consider the very question of what it means to change and what it means to be "the same," and, above all, how both states can be true at once. After all, when the child asks the piper to *sing* rather than *pipe* his song, the piper sings "the same again," leaving us to wonder how the song can be "the same" even as the very nature of the performance has also changed. Here too, at the close of the poem, a similar question is also raised by the shift in aesthetic medium: what does it mean to *hear* rather than *read* a book?

The most obvious answer to the question (that a child first comes to books by being read to, and so of course *hears* rather than *reads* a book) takes us only so far, and the poem invites us to go further. When, in the fourth stanza, the piper plucks "a hollow reed" and makes "a rural pen," we are inevitably tempted to think of a pen as a writing instrument. And yet a reed is also essential to a woodwind instrument precisely like the pipe or flute with which the poem begins – in fact, a "hollow reed" is, if you think about it, a much more accurate description of such an instrument than of a tool for writing (pens in Blake's day were invariably solid dip pens rather than hollow fountain pens, which came into broad use only later in the nineteenth century). If we abandon our inhibitions a little and follow the poem's lead, we can take up its invitation to think of writing and playing (and hence reading and hearing, sight and sound, also speech and writing) as two versions of the same thing, or rather two versions of something that is simultaneously the same and different – in fact, something that remains all the more "the same" the more it changes (*plus ça change*). And that in turn makes it less surprising to consider that one could *hear* rather than *read* a book, and indeed that one could *play* a book rather than simply *writing* one. Again, what had seemed to be a straight, even progressive, line leading from piping to writing turns out to be a circle, and we are back to where we started. This is not to mention, of course, that Blake refers to "my happy songs," and there are various reports that he did indeed sing them, to his own tunes (and in fact *Songs of Innocence and of Experience* have subsequently been set to music by a range of composers, including Vaughan Williams).

All this makes the poem sound rather playfully joyful, and we might even say innocent. But through its subtle use of language, it is also alerting us to a darker potential here, associated perhaps inevitably with a kind of writing (or is it playing?) that seems to require as a point of departure staining "the water clear," which suggests a kind of contamination, pollution, or corruption. Our sense that joy and cheer may be attended – tainted or haunted – by something darker is a feeling accentuated by the other meaning of "rural pen" lurking here, namely, a livestock enclosure, a space of confinement. Just as the act of production seems to necessitate also an act of defilation or negation (staining the water clear), so too does the expression of joy seem to be attended by a sense of confinement. On this note, having already invited us to think about the relation between writing and sound, the plate now seeks to connect us also from words and sounds to the visual field, as we see snaking across the bottom of the printed plate a pair of vines that does indeed seem to enclose the final stanza in a kind of pen.

The last thing I want to add to my reading of this text (really, these texts) is to point out that this shift to the visual field inevitably draws our attention not merely to the bottom of the plate, and for that matter the series of almost inscrutable designs (and those loops of vines) framing the words, but also to the neighboring plates. For the closest the book comes to illustrating – in a conventional sense – the Introduction to *Songs of Innocence* is actually not on the plate itself but on an altogether different plate: the frontispiece, where we see a piper looking up to a flying child (see Figure 1.2). And on a different plate still, the title page (see Figure 1.3), we see children reading (or hearing) a book; maybe this is even a picture of the book picturing itself being read/heard.

In any case, we can see now that these three plates (in the Introduction, the frontispiece, and the title page) are tied together. Each one directs us away from itself and toward the others, together with which it constitutes a kind of mini network, though a network that Blake constantly tinkered with as he produced copies of *Songs of Innocence*. And it's not just that these three plates constitute a network: some of the images on the plates, in particular the sheep in the background of the frontispiece, are echoed throughout the *Songs*, and indeed throughout Blake's work, all the way through *Jerusalem*. It is as though in reading any one of Blake's works, we are always being reminded of the links – repetitions that change – tying it to others.

What we have in the Introduction to *Songs of Innocence*, then, is a piece that encourages us to re-read, to read backward and sideways and in circles rather than simply forward in a straight line; a piece that, for all its careful investment in language, also always playfully teases us to think beyond the words on the printed page; a piece that encourages us to think about the relations among and between words, images, and sounds; and, finally, a piece that is always gesturing away from itself and toward other pieces (the frontispiece, the title page, other plates in the book, and beyond the book that pick up the same visual iconography and make it different precisely by coding it as the same). What we have, in other words, is a piece that encourages us to find meaning in movement rather than in containment in what we might indeed think of as a pen – and to think of a text as a charged and dynamic, ever-changing, ever-reconstituted, forcefield of relations among elements rather than a static, inert, lifeless object.

Having taken our cues and lessons for reading from the Introduction to *Songs of Innocence*, it's time to move on and see how they help us open up a reading approach to Blake's work more generally.

FIGURE 1.2. Frontispiece from *Songs of Innocence*, copy G, plate 1.

FIGURE 1.3.   Title page from *Songs of Innocence*, copy G, plate 2.

Here, a quick word is in order to explain what reading Blake generally entails these days. For many decades, the study of Blake's work was effectively split. On the one hand, there were scholars of the visual arts who worked on Blake's etchings, drawing, paintings, and indeed the illuminated books themselves seen as artworks. On the other, there were literary scholars (Northrop Frye and David Erdman among them) for whom Blake was primarily a poet whose books could be unproblematically stripped of their visual components and reproduced in carefully edited – and homogenized, standardized – volumes of complete works alongside letters, marginal notes, and other writings. Blake studies were revolutionized in the 1970s by the idea of seeing the work – and the illuminated books in particular – as constituting what W. J. T. Mitchell called a composite art, the verbal and visual features of which ought to be read alongside each other rather than in isolation. The field has since undergone two further revolutions: first (the scholarship of Robert Essick, Morris Eaves, Joseph Viscomi, and Michael Phillips constitutes essential reading here) through an intensification of the study of Blake's methods of printing and production, which has brought much greater attention to the material nature of the illuminated books, and especially to the enormous differences from copy to copy of particular plates and books; and, second, more recently still, through the increasing availability of high-quality facsimiles and reproductions of the illuminated books – especially the online Blake Archive – which has completely transformed the way Blake is now read, studied, and taught.

I am going to assume that you have access to one or another of these facsimiles as you develop your own reading of Blake's work. Simply to tell, to direct, you how to read Blake – in the sense of claiming that I have a key to decode this reference or that character in Blake's work – would, of course, be the most un-Blakean thing in the world, so I am not going to do that (although there are many books that purport to do so, which you can consult for yourself). Rather, I'd like to suggest some guidelines from which you can pick and choose, taking whatever you find opens up the most interesting and exciting readings of the books, and leaving behind whatever seems not so productive as you read the words and images and ponder their relationship to one another.

When we read Blake's work we are, as we have already seen, encountering a composite art indeed. In reading the components constituting each plate (let alone reading different copies or versions of each plate) and in following the relations tying each plate to others both within a single book and among other books by Blake, we are always tracing and retracing different – and often contradictory – interpretive paths. There are, of course, what appear to be stories and characters and historical references in Blake's work. But it's important to remember that even the most apparently straightforward story or narrative in Blake never simply unfolds in a straight line; it also doubles back on itself, circles around and connects to other narratives and stories. That is, Blake's works undermine and reject the very principle of smooth, linear time (a point we will return to at greater length in later chapters). To this already abundant sense of openness, the verbal, visual, and aural elements constituting each plate open up an endless range of reading possibilities, as we move from one component to another. These interpretive possibilities are amplified when, as is often the case, these elements seem not to align very clearly together, or when one element (the visual, say, or the aural – and Blake's poems are extraordinarily sensitive to subtle shifts in rhyme or meter, or sudden bursts of onomatopoeia or alliteration, such as the sun-flower's "who countest the steps of the sun") adds a dimension that is missing from the others.

If you look at the plate of "London" in *Songs of Experience*, for example (see Figure 1.4), you will see a youthful figure leading an old man either past or toward a doorway, and either across or into a beam of light (the latter is more evident in some copies of *Songs* than in others). Nowhere in the poem is there any hint as to who either of these figures might be, nor, similarly, is there any explanation of the figure warming his or her hands by a fire – or, depending on how you read it, setting a fire to symbolically burn through the printed page – in the bottom third of the plate. The gap between what is happening in the words and what is happening in whatever you take the pictures to be inevitably opens up an almost infinite interpretive space. (It is precisely in this sense that, as I said earlier, the pictures in Blake's work don't simply illustrate the words in a conventional sense).

And what goes for the relatively – but only relatively – straightforward *Songs of Innocence and of Experience* is all the more true in other and often more complex works. *The Book of Urizen*, for example, contains several plates (see Figure 1.5, for example) that have no words at all but instead contain relatively large-scale images, most, or perhaps all, of which are impossible to pin down definitively in relation to the rest of the verbal/visual text they interrupt, and many of which are quite impossible to pin down definitely even on their own terms. In every single copy of *Urizen*, these plates are bound in a different sequence, but even if they had not been, reading the book involves pondering those images in relation to each

FIGURE 1.4. "London" from *Songs of Experience*, copy L, plate 51.

FIGURE 1.5. Plate 21 from *Book of Urizen*, copy A.

other as well as in relation to the other components of the book. The result is the vast amplification of the interpretive possibilities offered by the words taken on their own, or the combination of words and images on the plates that include both.

We can add to this the many and often astonishing variations in feel, texture, and tone sustained by the aural qualities of Blake's texts as well as the emotional resonances activated by shading and color. The starkly beautiful monochromatic copies of *Jerusalem* or of *America*, for example, sustain very different feelings than the colored copies. And those feelings tend to almost literally color our emotional relationship with the text as we read it, and hence to channel or direct our interpretive approach to it. The same thing goes for different copies of *Songs*: reading more than one copy at the same time (something the Blake Archive makes possible for those unable to spend time in, say, the British Museum leafing through two or three copies of *Songs* at once) reveals the extent to which these differences in tone really do sustain very different reading experiences.

Indeed, the fullest experience of reading Blake comes from reading multiple different copies of the "same" book simultaneously, because that allows us to amplify even further the already abundant interpretive resonances and openness made available in each copy taken on its own. Our reading of "The Tyger," for instance, can now take into account the fact that in certain copies of *Songs of Experience*, the animal in question looks appropriately – cosmically – mysterious or ferocious, while in others he looks rather pathetically tame, if not altogether silly. Our reading of "The Little Black Boy " can grapple with the question of what it means that in certain copies of *Songs of Innocence* the erstwhile little black boy looks like an African child (see Figure 1.6), while in others he is colored like a little white boy (see Figure 1.7). Our reading of *The Book of Urizen* can sift through the significance of the different arrangements of the full-page designs as well as the presence or absence of various plates in different copies (only two copies include them all). Our reading of *America* can ponder what it means that in some copies the final few lines of plate 4 are present in some copies and missing in others (see Figures 1.8 and 1.9). And so on.

And what goes for variations and differences goes for forms of sameness as well, because, as we have already seen, sameness and difference in Blake are not binary opposites but rather extensions of one another, operating on a continuum. Consider that flock of sheep in the background of the frontispiece to *Songs of Innocence*. We see them again in "The Shepherd," which in many copies comes right after the Introduction; in "The Lamb," on the second plate of "Little Black Boy"; the frontispiece and other plates of *Songs of Experience*, and they appear also in *All Religions Are One*, *Jerusalem*, *Milton*, and various separate drawings by Blake. The question is, is this the same flock of sheep that reappears throughout these different works that span Blake's entire career? Or does Blake just happen to draw a

FIGURE 1.6.   "Little Black Boy" (continued), from *Songs of Innocence*, copy L.

For when our souls have learn'd the heat to bear
The cloud will vanish we shall hear his voice.
Saying: come out from the grove my love & care,
And round my golden tent like lambs rejoice.

Thus did my mother say and kissed me,
And thus I say to little English boy.
When I from black and he from white cloud free,
And round the tent of God like lambs we joy :

Ill shade him from the heat till he can bear,
To lean in joy upon our fathers knee.
And then Ill stand and stroke his silver hair.
And be like him and he will then love me.

FIGURE 1.7. "Little Black Boy" (continued), from *Songs of Innocence*, copy G, plate 30.

FIGURE 1.8.   Plate 4 from *America*, copy M.

flock of sheep in one particular way when he wants to represent sheep? To
answer the question, we have to consider that this recurring flock of sheep –
with all its unmistakable Christian significance – is far from the only image
that appears repeatedly in Blake's work. Images of individual sheep also
recur; so does the figure of a resting blacksmith (shown in the same pose in
The Song of Los and in *Jerusalem*, for instance), an old man on a staff (he's

FIGURE I.9. Preludium II from *America*, copy O, plate 4.

there in "London," for example, but recurs in many other works by Blake); and there is the figure of a crouching youth looking upward who recurs in almost exactly the same configuration in works spanning Blake's career (including *The Marriage of Heaven and Hell*, *America*, *Jerusalem*, and Blake's illustrations to Blair's *Grave*; see the discussion of this in Chapter 6, and also Figures 6.1–6.6). And so on again.

To these recycled images we can also add various lines of text that are repeated through Blake's different works. "Every thing that lives is holy," for example, is repeated in *The Marriage of Heaven and Hell*, *America*, *Visions of the Daughters of Albion*, and *The Four Zoas*, and "The Guardian Prince of Albion burns in his nightly tent" is both the first line of *America* and the last line of "Africa" in the *Song of Los*, suggesting a connection – a point of simultaneity or repetition, a sameness that changes – between those two seemingly distinct books. And there are textual as well as verbal echoes tying together different works: think of the paired "Nurse's Song," or "Holy Thursday," or "Chimney Sweeper" pieces in *Songs of Innocence and of Experience*; or, quite explicitly, of the way in which the narrator of "The Tyger" asks "Did he smile his work to see? / Did he who made the Lamb make thee?" Those lines are usually read as references to God, part of the cosmic mystery of "The Tyger," but they could also be read at a much more mundane level as referring to Blake himself reflecting on his own craftsmanship quite literally as the maker, in a material sense, of the two plates, "The Lamb" and "The Tyger." At the very least, the lines prompt us to reconsider the two pieces in terms of one another, rather than each solely on its own.

And it is exactly that kind of relation between distinct works that the repetition or recycling of verbal and visual elements throughout Blake's corpus pushes us to consider. Which brings us back to the question of what it means to repeat an image or a line, to reproduce it from one context to another.

To answer that question, we have to bear in mind that Blake was a professional engraver who was always working with images and indeed other kinds of texts, and their reproduction. In principle, the task of the commercial engraver was faithfully to reproduce a stream of identical copies of a single master original (a portrait, say, or a map, or a design of some kind), and indeed engravers were considered tradesmen rather than being granted the social status of artists precisely because their occupation was taken to be reproductive rather than original or conceptual – involving copying rather than creating. Although Blake's illuminated books were the products of exactly the same machinery used to produce conventional prints (including those commissioned from Blake himself), they turned this commercial logic on its head, as we have seen. And in the process, they altered beyond recognition the very logic separating the socially glorified conception of the Artist from the execution of the mere jobbing tradesman, and hence of course the exalted original from the mere copy.

For, exactly in the sense that a copy of one of Blake's books isn't really a copy in the ordinary sense of the term (because it is also simultaneously an original in its own right), the repeated "copies" of particular images or lines of text that we see reproduced throughout Blake's works are more than copies in the degraded sense of that term. They extend the play of sameness and difference that occurs in so many different registers through-out the work. For they are both the same and different, just as different copies of a particular plate or a particular illuminated book are also both the same and different. In this case, too, the subtle subversion of identity and difference helps to undermine the autonomy of any given line or image or plate or copy and tie it all the more closely together into a network of other, simultaneously identical and different, lines, images, plates, and copies spanning the length of Blake's career. You may be reading this line or looking at this image, but it's never really *just* this line or this image – it's always also part of a greater unity. You may be reading the "Chimney Sweeper" in *Innocence*, but you are also in some way reading the "Chimney Sweeper" of *Experience*. You may be reading *America* or the *Visions* or the *Marriage* or the *Song of Los*, but you are also in some sense reading the other books too, and those recycled and repeated, simultaneously same and different, words and images are there to remind you of the links tying the different copies of each to the others, and each work to the others as well.

That is, some of the interpretive work that occurs in our engagement with Blake's texts is the product of this sense of disarticulation, decentral-ization, and openness, which is why I noted earlier that Blake's work encourages us to find meaning not simply in a text seen as a static object requiring decoding – a narrative unfolding in smooth linear time – but in the backward, forward, sideways, and circular movement among the elements constituting the text as an ever-shifting forcefield. So, when we move back and forth among the lines of the poem, or from words to sounds, or from sounds to pictures, or from one copy of "the same" plate to another, or from one plate to another, or, for that matter, from one of Blake's books to another, we are tracing something that is as important to the very meaning of the text itself as the story it seems to tell. How Blake's texts work, as Nelson Hilton once put it, is very much part of what they mean.[2]

For this movement away from the words on the surface of the printed page is what helps generate and sustain our reading as we shift our engagement with Blake's text, and even as we alter our understanding of what the text is, from a set of (themselves already indeterminate) printed words on the page to a set of unstable, ever-varying relations among and between different elements including sound and the visual field on the one hand, and, on the other hand, other plates within the same book or indeed other books altogether. Every time we encounter the text, in other words, we are encountering something that is both the same *and* different: the same, in that the elements enabling it remain "the same"; and different, in that we trace different interpretive paths on every encounter with those elements, which also always change. This is one of the reasons that each of the diminutive and seemingly innocuous *Songs of Innocence* constantly yields, or rather makes available, new readings, interpretations, and meanings. For we are dealing here with a text that sees "the same" as always different, and that regards identity as difference itself.

It is exactly in this respect that we need to always return, in reading Blake, and ground ourselves in the material fact that *Songs of Innocence and of Experience* exists not as a master concept executed in a series of identically – that is, slavishly, mechanically, faithfully, blindly – reproduced copies, but rather in multiple *non-identical* copies, so non-identical that every single copy is different, and yet they are *also* all "the same again." For we see at work here a notion – that identity and difference can be seen as continuous rather than read in opposition to one another – that lies right at the very heart of everything Blake ever did, and it is a notion to which we will repeatedly return in later chapters. For, as we shall see, just as a book for Blake is not a closed, contained body, but rather a collection of moving particles that are at certain moments shared in common with other moving particles, so too are other forms of identity, including ourselves.

CHAPTER 2

Text

There are striking theological and political implications to Blake's engagement with the idea of an open and decentralized text, a text that encourages us to generate meanings as we move among and between the elements of which it is composed rather than seeking to make us submit to its unilateral dictates, or forcing us to treat it as a sacred object to be decoded according to a set of interpretive principles revealed only to (or by) a priestly or scholarly hierarchy. For, whatever else it may be, how we imagine or conceive of the relationship between reading and authority is also inevitably a political question. The notion that authority is grounded in a text, the idea that authority can be conferred by reading, possessing, or claiming to possess the special or hidden knowledge to read a text, the belief that there exists a monopoly on interpretation available only to some (an initiated and licensed elite) and not to others – these all rather easily lend themselves to restrictive, not to say coercive, forms of both doctrine and politics. Whereas the contrary notion that reading and interpretation are open to all, and that authority is something to avoid – or at best to share, rather than to aspire to – lends itself to very different and inherently more inclusive and democratic ideas of both religion and politics.

These contrasting notions of textuality, authority, and the politics of reading were central to the theological and political controversies of the seventeenth century from which Blake derived many of his ideas, including his disavowal of elitist textual politics and his contrary interest in forms of reading open to all. ("Christ & his Apostles were Illiterate Men," he notes, not members of the educated elite; he adds that "the Beauty of the Bible is that the most Ignorant & Simple Minds Understand it Best.")[1] After all, the English Revolution had challenged and disrupted long-established religious and political monopolies, especially those of the monarchy. The unprecedented moment of theological and intellectual liberty following the execution of King Charles I in 1649 had enabled all kinds of ideas to flourish, including radical notions of political and religious freedom that were profoundly linked to and motivated by democratizing readings of the New Testament that defied the doctrines of the established church hierarchy.

Those years also saw the emergence of England's first sustained campaign for a recognizably modern form of democracy (notably in the Leveller movement), and of communist projects calling for the collective ownership of property on the basis of radical religious principles such as the idea of a community of being. "The earth was made by Almighty God, to be a common treasury of livelihood for whole mankind in all his branches, without respect of persons," wrote the seventeenth-century communist Gerrard Winstanley, just as "whole mankind was made equall, and knit into one body by one spirit of love."[2] Countless radical intellectuals and sects, including the followers of Winstanley as well as Anabaptists, Familists, Muggletonians, and those derisively termed by their enemies the Ranters, emerged in this moment of liberty (which flourished until Oliver Cromwell imposed a new kind of order on the country, violently suppressing the intellectual, religious, and political freedoms unleashed by the Revolution). Many openly preached a gospel of joyous sharing, mutual commitment, and doctrines of antinomian equality and freedom – that is, freedom not just *before* but *from* the law and the established church – which would be echoed in Blake's work over a century later, from the Little Vagabond's plea in *Songs of Experience* ("If at the Church they would give us some Ale. / And a pleasant fire, our souls to regale; / We'd sing and we'd pray, all the live-long day; / Nor ever once wish from the Church to stray")[3] to the later complexities of *The Four Zoas* and *Jerusalem*.

It should hardly come as a surprise that many of the ideas that exploded on the scene in seventeenth-century England are explicitly echoed in Blake's own work. For one thing, some of these ideas were also important to writers who experienced the English Revolution firsthand and went on to influence Blake. These include John Bunyan (whose *Pilgrim's Progress* inspired a beautiful series of illustrations by Blake) and, above all, John Milton: a defender of intellectual freedom, a staunch republican, and, as Blake puts it in *The Marriage of Heaven and Hell*, "a true poet, and of the Devils party without knowing it," that is, someone whose dedication to the cause of freedom exceeded even his own consciousness of it.[4]

Apart from their literary manifestations, however, these radical ideas were also maintained and transmitted in unorthodox forms of religious faith and political belief that extended from the seventeenth century into the eighteenth, to which Blake had personal connections as a devout

Christian who remained outside the Church of England, professing scorn for what he called "state religion."[5] They seemed again to explode upon the scene in the moment of revolutionary transformation heralded by the French Revolution, which many in England saw as the harbinger of a new era of radical equality, justice, and freedom, and even as a replay of England's own seventeenth-century revolution. Thus these recycled ideas returned to the center of political and religious debate in Blake's lifetime. For example, the political positions articulated by seventeenth-century Levellers (primarily their call for universal male suffrage) were picked up point by point by reformers and radicals in London and elsewhere in the immediate aftermath of the French Revolution and became commonplace (and indeed ultimately institutionalized in the great reform acts of the nineteenth century). In the meantime, many of the unorthodox religious pamphlets that had first seen the light of the day in the turbulent 1650s – and had seemed to some to have been all but forgotten, hidden, or lost after the Restoration – were dusted off and reprinted in fresh editions in the 1790s, as though their time had come (again).

Thus it is no coincidence that some of the notions most consistently articulated in Blake's illuminated books have such a strikingly seventeenth-century feel to them. The full historical significance of the claim, in *The Marriage of Heaven and Hell*, that "God only Acts & Is, in existing beings or Men,"[6] or of Blake's repeated insistence that "every thing that lives is holy,"[7] becomes apparent when these lines are read alongside their seventeenth-century antecedents, such as the Ranter Jacob Bauthumley's assertion that God is the substance and being "of all Creatures and things, and fills Heaven and Earth and all other places" and hence that God "hath his Being no where else out of the Creatures"; that is, precisely as Blake puts it, that he exists immanently "in existing beings or Men" rather than independently of them in a transcendent form.[8] Throughout his work, Blake repeatedly returns to this and other ideas that were central to antinomian belief, including – as in this case – the principle of immanence, which, as we saw in the previous chapter, proves as vital to understanding the material and formal dimension of Blake's work as it does to reading the work at an interpretive level.

Blake had his own investments in many of the ideas coming out of the seventeenth century, then, and he adapted them to new purposes in his work from the 1790s and on into the nineteenth century. We will return to some of these ideas in later chapters, in our reading of Blake's understanding of desire and selfhood, his understanding of making (making art, making prints, making poetry, making life itself), and both his religious and political positions on the mobilization of faith against power. In the remainder of this chapter, however, I want to explore how some of these beliefs play a role in Blake's deployment and understanding of textuality, particularly his sense of the relationship between texts and authority. Following the example established in the previous chapter, I want to do so by grounding our exploration in a reading of a particular text from *Songs of Innocence and of Experience* – "The Garden of Love" (see Figure 2.1).

> I went to the Garden of Love,
> And saw what I never had seen:
> A Chapel was built in the midst,
> Where I used to play on the green.
> And the gates of this Chapel were shut,
> And Thou shalt not. writ over the door;
> So I turned to the Garden of Love,
> That so many sweet flowers bore,
> And I saw that it was filled with graves,
> And tomb-stones, where flowers should be:
> And Priests in black gowns, were walking their rounds,
> And binding with briars, my joys & desires.

As is so often the case in Blake's work, the seemingly obvious way to read the poem may not yield the most fruitful results, even if there is nothing necessarily wrong with it as far as it goes. At face value, certainly, what seems to be staged here is a contrast between, on the one hand, the freedom of love, joy, and desire and, on the other, the forms of restraint set into practice by building, writing, and binding; or in other words a contrast between openness and closure: the life of the garden and the death of writing and the grave. The most obvious form of writing here (obvious because it so expressly calls attention to itself) is the commandment, neatly tied, via that misplaced period in the middle of the sixth line, with writ, or in other words legal writing, royal writing, tyrannical, authoritative, would-be divine, or monarchical writing – writing as the expression of power, and ultimately of death.

This version of writing seeks among other things to displace and negate any other kind of writing, as though to write is necessarily to command, to write is to issue a writ. In aiming for unilateral and inescapable or omniscient control, writing as commandment seems – or wants – to be all-encompassing. It's precisely in this claim of omniscience, however, that the power of writing as commandment starts to break down, as we recognize that "Thou shalt not" is actually a remarkably open and capacious

FIGURE 2.1. "The Garden of Love," from *Songs of Experience*, Copy L, plate 45.

commandment: thou shalt not – *what*? *Anything*? In seeking to proscribe everything, strangely enough, the commandment actually ends up proscribing nothing at all; in overreaching, it reveals its bankruptcy. This kind of textual power turns out to be powerless, in other words, or rather its potency exists only to the extent that you accept that it does: only to the extent that you fill in the blank of the missing verb to complete the commandment, "thou shalt not . . . " and behave accordingly. "God only Acts & Is, in existing beings or Men," indeed!

What then of the Garden of Love as the seeming alternative to the structured, literally ordering, power of the commanding text and of the figures of power and authority Blake invariably associates with it – including for instance "God & his Priest & King"[9] decried by the Chimney Sweeper elsewhere in *Songs of Experience*? Much of how we read the poem depends on how we understand the significance of the line "I saw what I never had seen." It could be that the narrator is seeing something entirely new, that is, a built structure that has been imposed, created on the green where he used to play. But it could also be – in fact I would say that it's more likely to be – that the narrator is suddenly recognizing something that has been there all along, but that he had not noticed before: that the flowers among which he thought he had been playing were in fact really all along graves and tombstones, and it is just now that he is realizing his misreading of his own situation. It's especially in this connection that life seems so sharply contrasted with death, and by extension that life seems aligned with freedom and play, flowers and love, as opposed to writing as commandment, restraint, and ultimately death. It is also precisely in this connection, however – where the song seems at its darkest as we see death and restriction apparently closing off and choking away play, life, desire, and joy – that a whole new train of associations is opened up, and with it not simply a brighter conclusion but also one that helps us more adequately to understand the relationship between writing and power, texts and authority, in Blake.

For there is a recurring series of relationships between writing and the grave that we see at work throughout Blake's work, and not only in *Songs of Experience*. At around the time he was wrapping up *Songs of Experience* in 1794, he picked up the first of several drawing or engraving projects to illustrate poems or books of poetry associated with death and the grave, namely, Edward Young's *Night Thoughts* (the edition illustrated by Blake would be published in 1797). Shortly afterward, he produced illustrations for Thomas Gray's *Elegy Written in a Country Church-Yard*, and a few years later for Robert Blair's *The Grave*. All of these projects speak to

Blake's ongoing interest in the relationship between life and death, and in particular the relationship between death – and especially graves – and writing. That, after all, is the primary theme in Gray's *Elegy*, which repeatedly returns to the question of the relationship between writing, death, and memorialization, contrasting the fragile temporariness of life, sound, and aurality with the apparent permanence of writing.

Blake would have found Gray's meditation on these questions fascinating, but he had his own take on them as well. It comes up, for instance, not only in "The Garden of Love" but also in another of the *Songs of Experience*, "The Little Girl Lost," which begins as follows: "In futurity / I prophetic see, / That the earth from sleep, / (Grave the sentence deep) / Shall arise and seek / For her maker meek." The parenthesis contained in that fourth line, (Grave the sentence deep), is worthy of a chapter on its own! It can be read of course as a reference to the gravity of the sentence in question, but, because it interrupts the lines among which it is embedded, a more fruitful reading of the line involves seeing it in rather more literal terms, perhaps even as a kind of tombstone-like memorialization in writing, speech turned into writing – a kind of note of Blake talking to himself, telling himself to grave the sentence deep as he etched the plate. For to grave, for Blake, *is* to write. So *of course* there is in his mind a relationship between writing and the grave.

Engraving involves digging into – en-graving – the surface of a copper plate. To be more precise, in conventional commercial engraving, the designs are planted beneath the surface of the plate, springing to life in ink on the paper during the printing process, which pulls the ink out of the engraved lines and on to the paper on which it is printed. In the form of relief etching Blake used in producing the illuminated books, it's the background that is burned away, revealing the words and designs in relief, but nevertheless there is a similar play of surface and depth at stake: it is by going beneath the surface that words and images are brought to life above the surface, in ink on paper, in both engraving and relief etching. This takes us back to that parenthesis in the fourth line of "Little Girl Lost": although it is embedded in the flow of the text, it doesn't quite interrupt the very sentence whose gravity it seeks to accentuate by virtue of the fact that it is enclosed – engraved, entombed – within its own closure as defined by the parentheses themselves; it is as though that line exists in parallel with the sentence, alongside it, or even, in a way, beneath it. It reminds us of the relationship between surface and depth, and indeed opposites in general, throughout Blake's work, and in particular the generative, fruitful, productive, and, dare I say it, *playful* relationship between writing and the grave. In Blake's work, all sentences and all forms of life come from the grave. Thus it's no coincidence that the next line of "Little Girl Lost," after "(Grave the sentence deep)," is "Shall arise and spring . . . ," for the grave in Blake is as much the site of resurrection and rebirth as it is the site of death and burial (see the discussion of this theme in Chapter 6).

If we return with this insight to "The Garden of Love," one point that becomes clearer is that the opposition between life and death, and hence between writing and the grave, is less stark or rigid than it might have seemed at first glance. Just as digging and planting produce the garden, engraving produces the sentence. Life and death are not opposites; they exist on a continuum, the one producing the other. But there is more still to be added, especially as we bring the plate's design into the discussion (see Figure 2.1). There we see a priest apparently teaching two children, instructing them in how to read. He holds a book in his hand; lacking books, they mimic his stance, clasping their hands in prayer. What is reading for him, in other words, is empty prayer – mere imitative supplication – for them; imitative because only he has access to the text, and what they are given depends entirely on the reading he provides to them as a licensed authority of the church. A certain form of reading, we might say, involves reverence, blind following, devotion to the text (or at least the appearance of that authority – for all we know, the children may be subversively mimicking the priest). As we saw in the previous chapter, however, there are other forms of reading that transfer agency to the reader from the text and involve far more effort on the reader's part, and hence freedom, play.

This brings us back to the question with which I opened this chapter, namely, the contrast between a decentralized text, or we might say an immanent form of textuality, one that encourages us to generate meanings as we trace our own repeatedly diverging paths among the elements of which it is composed, as opposed to the kind of text that seeks to make us submit to its commandments and dictates, precisely as in, "thou shalt not." In a sense, "The Garden of Love" aims to express the principles of love, play, joy, and freedom with which we would like to associate Blake's work. But it all seems so hopeless. When we see the church displacing the garden of love, or the cleric in the design teaching – trapping, tricking? – those children, instructing them in blind reverence to the printed text the reading and interpretation of which remains his prerogative, and above all when we see the priests in black gowns walking their rounds, the plate seems hopelessly bleak, as though the struggle for freedom in the face of authority has been lost.

But it is precisely in the moment of defeat that we see the tables being turned. For where is "The Garden of Love?" The poem, I mean – the verbal text of the plate? It is *in* the very grave toward which the priest is gesturing with his left hand in the design. It is supposed to have been safely contained, the poem itself, like our joys and desires, literally bound with briars (more visible in some versions of the plate than in others) and buried beneath the surface. But there it is, not merely enduring, but ready to spring to life all over again as we read it *in spite of* the forms of restriction and proscription that had condemned it to the briar-bound grave.

It ought to be clearer than ever by now that dictatorial logic, the logic of commandment, and the textual politics associated with it (that of reverence and blind commitment, of devotion and submission to authority) are never as all-encompassing and powerful as they claim or pretend to be. The very text that seeks to operate in terms of a logic of commandment and authority can contain within itself its very opposite, and hence the seeds of its own destruction and overturning, allowing us, like the narrator, to see what we never had seen, even if it really was there all along. Like life and death, or writing and the grave, the two forms of textuality involved in open as opposed to closed reading, exist not in stark opposition or negation of one another, but rather on a continuum, bound up with one another even within the same text.

The text itself may be seen as the site of a struggle between these different approaches, these different understandings of textual politics, these different configurations of the relationship between texts and authority, the results of which alternately turn flowers into tombstones or tombstones into flowers (in this context it's worth taking a look at that Memorable Fancy in *The Marriage of Heaven and Hell* where the narrator accompanies an Angel through a church vault, and each projects on to the world a vision intended to "impose" on the other. The Angel projects a terrifying vision intended to cow the narrator into submission, while the narrator sees, in the Angel's absence, only "a pleasant bank beside a river by moon light hearing a harper who sung to the harp."[10] This reminds us that in Blake's work the landscapes and spaces – the very realities – we inhabit are always generated and sustained either by our own imagination or by our submission to the imagination of others.)[11] Some texts, then, may want to make us believe in and accept the dictates of a unilateral, closed reading, while others may actively and playfully encourage us to read openly, but ultimately any text can be read either way. Even a text that seeks to command and extract subservience and blind faith, to impose itself on us via the logic of commandment, is open to subversion and other kinds of reading, as "The Garden of Love" reminds us.

The contrast between these two approaches to reading, these two
conceptions of the politics of interpretation, is a recurring theme in Blake's
work. It is framed most explicitly in antinomian terms, and, at that, in
explicit reference to the seventeenth-century Revolution, in Blake's manuscript work *The Everlasting Gospel*, the very title of which refers directly to
one of the central conceptions of the antinomian heresies of the seventeenth century, in which the idea of an everlasting gospel – animated by a
logic of love and forgiveness rather than of commandment and punishment – plays a central role. Blake's *Everlasting Gospel* is, among other
things, a meditation on different approaches to reading, but it doesn't
merely oppose the blind obedience associated with commandment to the
freedom of open and joyous reading: it insists that both logics can be, or
perhaps inevitably are, contained in the same text, including the Bible
itself. "Both read the Bible day & night," Blake concludes his manuscript;
"But thou readst black where I read white."[12] Here the opposition between
black and white refers not so much to their apparent symbolic significance
(good versus evil, for instance) but rather much more literally – and only
then metaphorically – to the black-and-white of a conventionally printed
text, or in other words to the contrast between an approach to textuality
that takes the printed word including its logic of commandment for
granted (hence seeing only the black ink of the word, taking it at face
value) as opposed to an approach to reading that looks between the lines,
between the words, around them, beneath them, taking in the hidden
background (symbolized by the white of the page upon which the black
ink is imposed), and reading the text, as it were, against the grain, even
against itself, seeking out its forms of prohibition and proscription, the
very things banished by the "Thou shalt not."

The tension between these approaches to the relationship between texts
and authority is a recurring theme in Blake's work, nowhere more clearly than
in *The Book of Urizen*, which Blake first printed in 1794. This has long
been seen by scholars as a critique of the Bible, and in particular of Genesis
(down to its double-columned printing format and chapter headings, which
clearly mimic the King James or Authorized Version), if not altogether a kind
of anti-Bible. *The Book of Urizen* is, I would argue, more generally a book
critical of books. Or, to be more precise, it is a book about the kind of book
that would seek to command us how to read, that would try to impose on us
its own interpretation of itself (and indeed of the world around us). Hence,
it is a critique of that mode of textuality – registered by the "Thou shalt not"
in "The Garden of Love" – that operates by way of a closed and restrictive
logic of commandment, and, by extension, of that mode of politics that

similarly operates according to the logic of despotism and command. The key figure here is Urizen, who can be thought of as the embodiment of the baleful logic of command and dictatorship, almost literally its condensation into a single body: an event which, among other things, the *Book of Urizen* itself seeks to document. He thus stands also for that understanding of God as a tyrannical, despotic taskmaster (as opposed to the loving, joyous, and immanently constituted understanding of God that we also see in Blake, to which we will return at greater length in later chapters).

Indeed, the running theme of *The Book of Urizen* is Urizen's will, his attempt, to impose his authority on the world around him. Coming into being in a formless world (formless in the sense that it lacks individual forms of being until his sudden arrival precipitates individuality), his dream is to organize life, to bring all life under the control of "One command, one joy, one desire, / One curse, one weight, one measure, / One King, one God, one Law."[13] This involves above all the regulation and limitation, the stunting, of our formerly infinite capacities; or in other words our transformation into individual bodies and selves through the narrowing of our ability to perceive: quite literally the re-engineering of our bodies and minds and our reduction to highly regulated forms of existence, "bound down / To earth by their narrowing perceptions," and hence unable to "rise at will / In the infinite void," as had been the case formerly.[14] We will come back to what all this means for our bodies and selves in a later chapter, but what I want to mark for now is what this kind of regulation means for texts, books, and reading.

For Urizen's will to control the world is expressed – of course – in books: books that seek to bind and control our joys and desires. "Here alone I in books formd of metals / Have written the secrets of wisdom / The secrets of dark contemplation," he proclaims. "Lo!" he adds shortly later, "I unfold my darkness: and on / This rock, place with strong hand the Book / of eternal brass, written in my solitude. / Laws of peace, of love, of unity: / Of pity, compassion, forgiveness."[15] One of the plates of the *Book of Urizen* (see Figure 2.2) shows Urizen revealing his book of brass; it is one of the images with the greatest range of variations among Blake's illuminated books, with each copy (see Figures 2.3, 2.4, and 2.5 for example) conveying its own distinct impression of the book of brass – gold or brass in one copy, black in another, mixed in a third, multicolored, blue, white, and so on in others, and with an ever-changing array of gibberish scripts and symbols. Even as a weapon of dictatorship, the book of command constantly slips out of its own control, its very insistence on singularity always sliding into variability, multiplicity, and difference.

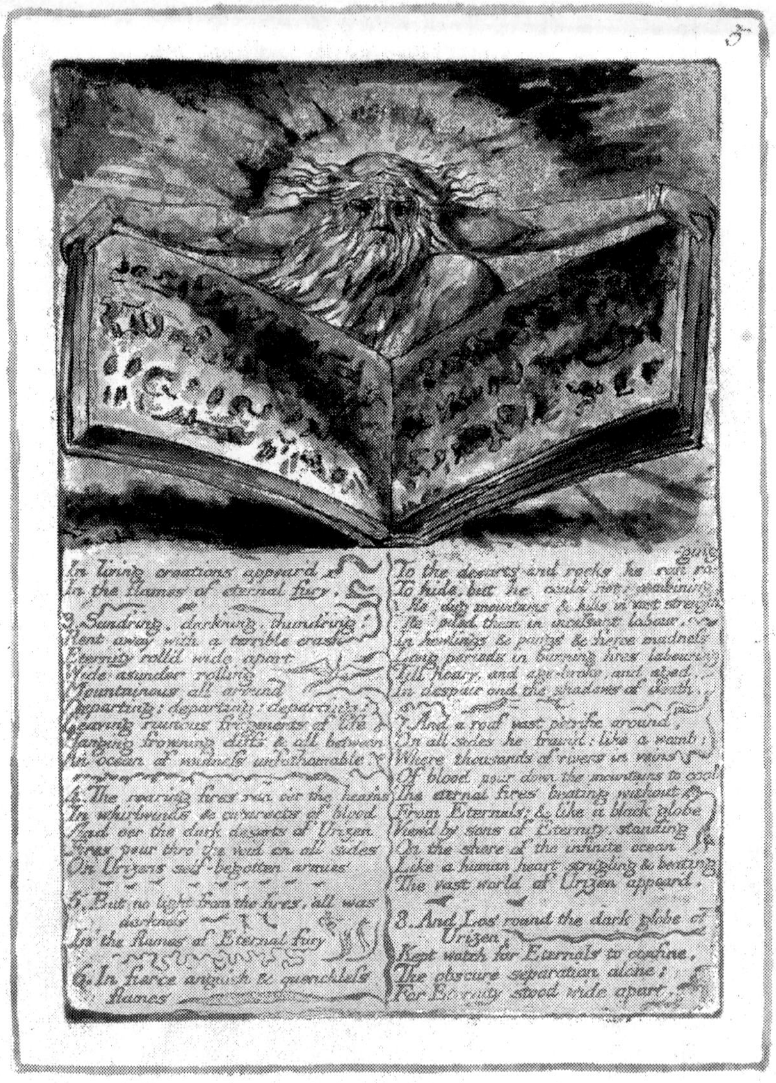

FIGURE 2.2. Object 5 (Bentley 5, Erdman 5) from *Book of Urizen*, Copy G.

In other works, notably *The Four Zoas*, but also *Europe* and the *Song of Los*, we see (and hear) Urizen tinkering with and adjusting his books, reading them out loud and in fact trying to assert control through reading, dictating. The point, however, is that, even armed with his metal books,

FIGURE 2.3. *Book of Urizen*, Copy A, plate 8.

Urizen is ultimately unable to impose his will and his logic of commandment on the world, which always, over and again, and at every level, slips
out of his control. Sickened, he curses "Both sons and daughters; for he
saw / That no flesh nor spirit could keep / His iron laws one moment."[16]

FIGURE 2.4.   *Book of Urizen*, Copy C, plate 6.

Just as we saw in "The Garden of Love," then, the textual logic of commandment inevitably also fails in *The Book of Urizen*. This brings us back to the question of what it means for it to be a book critiquing the concept of the book. The critique unfolds on at least three levels at once.

FIGURE 2.5. *Book of Urizen*, Copy D, plate 4.

First, as we have just seen, it unfolds in terms of the narrative of Urizen's abject failure to impose his will and his Law on the world through dictation and books, no matter how ironclad they may be. Second, there are several designs in *The Book of Urizen* that offer visual meditations on the question of the book, beginning with the title page (see Figure 2.6),

FIGURE 2.6.   *Book of Urizen*, Copy A, plate 1.

where we see a blind Urizen writing – or rather, literally, blindly copying – his books simultaneously with both hands at once, with another book at his feet and, in the background, the stone tablets of the Ten Commandments: the very antithesis of the Everlasting Gospel.

This is an image of dictatorship in overdrive: a blind despotism seeking to command and order as though only for the sake of commandment and ordering rather than with any more intelligent purpose in mind – and hence it is an image of the bankruptcy and emptiness of the logic of command and dictatorship (in every sense of that term) in the first place. Furthermore, going back to that series of images of Urizen revealing his book of brass, the extent to which each and every copy of *The Book of Urizen* reveals that image in a different style, color, or form (see Figures 2.2–2.5 again for examples) serves to emphasize the total lack of uniformity, the lack of ironclad rigidity, in any kind of book, no matter how despotic or authoritative it may claim to be. The irony here is that a book intended to enforce singularity and despotic unity is subversively illustrated in endless variations.

There are also several designs (see Figures 2.7 and 2.8, for example) in *The Book of Urizen* that show figures, including Urizen himself, pushing at the edges, the sides, and even the middle of the page, figuratively pushing the limits of the book and even in several instances all but pushing through the book – as though the designs themselves could somehow push through the printed page, or burn through it, or cause the book to self-destruct and burst into flames. Had he had different technologies to hand – or, if you can imagine this, access to some Hollywood studio's special effects warehouse – Blake would perhaps have made self-destroying versions of the *Book of Urizen*, ones that would melt down, dissolve, disintegrate, or explode after having been read. For the point of the book is to explode the very logic of the book itself; or at least the logic of the book conceived as the embodiment and formalization of a certain mode of textuality, writing, reading, commandment.

The Book of Urizen also formally subverts the logic of the book by refusing as much as possible to act like a book in the normal sense. Of the eight known copies of the book, only two contain all the plates. In each and every single copy, the plates containing only designs appear in a different sequence. Some copies have two chapter IVs; others have one. There are countless variations, inclusions, and exclusions of particular lines or small details or elements of the design from copy to copy to copy. As I pointed out in the previous chapter, all of Blake's illuminated books contain these kinds of variations to some extent, but none to such an extreme as in this case. *The Book of Urizen*, in short, pushes the very logic of the book to the breaking point, and arguably well beyond. A book about the book's will to power and commandment, it is itself, in effect, an un-book. And that of course is the third and final moment – the culmination – of its devastating critique of the form and concept of the book.

FIGURE 2.7.   *Book of Urizen*, Copy A, plate 13.

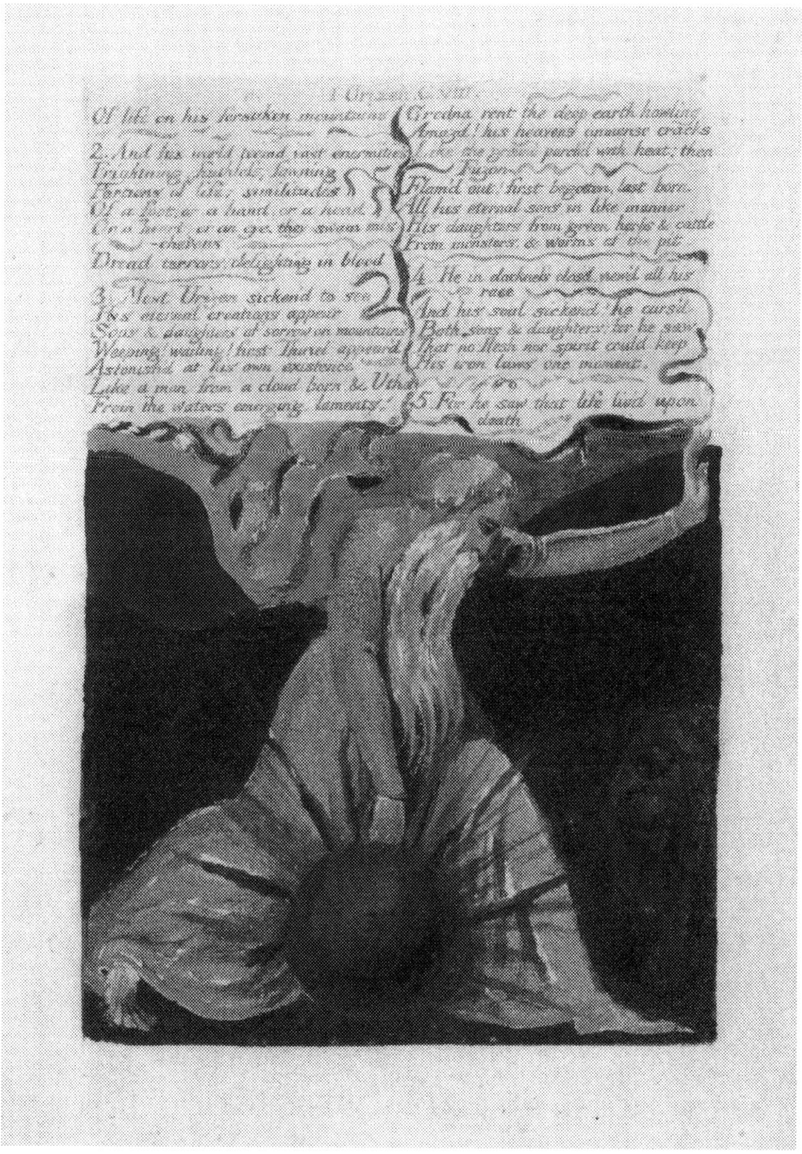

FIGURE 2.8. *Book of Urizen*, Copy A, plate 24.

Nor is *The Book of Urizen* the only candidate for an un-book among Blake's works. Another is *The Marriage of Heaven and Hell*, which Blake produced in 1790. Like *The Book of Urizen*, *The Marriage* pushes the boundaries of book definition to their limits and beyond. Quite apart from the usual endless variations characterizing Blake's illuminated books, what we call *The Marriage of Heaven and Hell* is actually three very distinct books or sub-books. We have, first of all, several copies of the more or less complete version of *The Marriage* in twenty-seven plates. Then there are two extant copies (copy L and copy M), in stand-alone pamphlet format, of the "Song of Liberty" that constitutes the last three plates of the full version of *The Marriage*. And there is another stand-alone pamphlet version (copy K) of four plates (the ones right before "The Song of Liberty") of the full version as well. These pamphlet versions of *The Marriage* were each printed monochrome, on a single, folded leaf of paper, precisely along the lines of the countless streams of handbills printed by radical activists or organizations in the heady revolutionary days of the 1790s.

Blake clearly thought of *The Marriage*, in one way or another, either as a modular book, bits and pieces of which could be broken off and printed into their own particular existence; or, the other way around, as an amalgamation of different constituent elements, elements that, even in the "complete" version of the text, never really cohere into a single, straightforward narrative.

Because of this built-in modularity, *The Marriage of Heaven and Hell* is in fact the single most emphatic expression of the mode of reading and textual politics with which all of Blake's works experiment to a greater or lesser degree, and the modularity carries over into both formal and generic dimensions as well. The complete text – though we have to wonder quite what one might mean by "complete" in this context – consists of many different generic forms and structures, both in poetry and in prose, spoken in several different voices and from a number of different and mutually contradictory points of view. Sometimes the narrative voice operates in the prophetic mode ("As a new heaven is begun, and it is now thirty-three years since its advent: the Eternal Hell revives"), sometimes in a personal one ("As I was walking among the fires of hell, delighted with the enjoyments of Genius; which to Angels look like torment and insanity . . . "). Sometimes it reads like a manifesto, sometimes like a travelogue, sometimes like a philosophical treatise, sometimes like a book of literary criticism – and sometimes like the disordered notes of a madman or a criminal genius.

The Marriage takes us from an account of the earliest forms of religion to a meditation on how we create the spaces we inhabit either through the exercise or the incapacitation of our imaginations, leading us along the way through a series of aphorisms on the conduct of everyday life, a sly but sympathetic critique of Milton's *Paradise Lost*, a digression on illuminated printing, a devastating attack on, first, the strange Swedish mystic Emmanuel Swedenborg, and, second, the established church and its affiliations with state power in England, before finally ending with a revolutionary call to arms that, we can be quite sure, would only have left most of the revolutionaries of Blake's London baffled and scratching their heads.

Because of the modularity of *The Marriage*, because of the jarring and discordant shifts from one mode, voice, style, genre, and form to another, and because of the absence of a single overarching structure, it is – if not from moment to moment then certainly overall – quite impossible to know how to read it; that is, what kind of approach to take to the text: is it serious? Humorous? Ironic? Funny? Subversive? Insane? Or each and all of these to some extent or another, at one time or another? Ultimately, *The Marriage* rebuffs any attempt to impose order on it; even when it seems to be barking orders or making prophetic pronouncements, it nevertheless resists reduction to a single interpretive stream; it is impossible to say it *means* this or is *about* that. It insists that we read it by dipping in and out, connecting this image or concept or line or insight to that, and to others throughout Blake's corpus (to which *The Marriage* has many explicit references and links), and making these connections, tracing these interpretive paths, over and over again in an endlessly shifting, kaleidoscope-like pattern of readings. There is no priesthood, no scholarly elite, that can possibly claim to possess the keys to hold a monopoly on its interpretation; it utterly refuses to be subject to that kind of reduction and containment, to allow the joys and desires it expresses to be bound with briars and buried alive.

Even more than *The Book of Urizen*, then, *The Marriage of Heaven and Hell* is the ultimate un-book. It refuses the very possibility of a self-enclosed, self-referential logic – the logic of commandment and the mode of reading necessarily associated with it – and insists instead on the need for us to trace and re-trace our own interpretive paths by linking together the bits and pieces, the constituent elements, of which it is immanently composed. In short, it embodies Blake's textual politics, it expresses the most fully articulated version of his approach to the relationship between texts and authority – it teaches us how to read in the spirit of Blake.

CHAPTER 3

Desire

I want to begin this chapter by going back to the discussion in the previous chapter of the "joys and desires" we see being bound by the priests in black gowns walking their rounds in "The Garden of Love." It has become commonplace to view the invocation of joy and desire both here and elsewhere in Blake's work as a reference to the attributes of an individual self, and even, perhaps, as an expression of selfishness. It's true, of course, that in this case the poem itself seems to invite precisely such an interpretation, since, at least at face value, the lines are indeed spoken by a narrator expressing his joys and desires (or rather expressing his fear of their restriction by others). But we need to be careful because both joy and desire consistently appear throughout Blake's work – where they are among the most frequently used terms – in connection to collective rather than merely individual experiences, suggesting that selfishness is not exactly what is at stake in them.

Moreover, even in *Songs of Innocence*, let alone the more complex later works such as *The Book of Urizen* or *The Four Zoas*, no reference to the individual self offers as stable a point of reference as might seem to be the case. This is an especially tricky point for those of us who read Blake's work from the standpoint of a culture and society steeped in discourses of selfish, competitive individualism. It's all too easy for us to take individual selfhood for granted as a point of departure for reading. It's also easy for us to lose sight of the history of the very notion of possessive individualism, and in particular its emergence and formation in precisely the same seventeenth-century moment that also gave rise to many other ways of imagining our being in rather more open and expansive terms – including, as we shall see, ones that were far more interesting to Blake than mere individuality. Any time we see what seems to be an individual self, an individual character, or even a narrative "I," in Blake's work, then, we have to be wary, careful not to automatically read it as the expression of an autonomous form of agency of the kind we have come to take for granted in our own twenty-first-century consumer culture.

All of this is to say that individual names in Blake's work don't necessarily mean what they often do in other works. An individual name often is little more than a placeholder, a temporary marker for a dynamic cluster of forces that will soon move on. Thus, for instance, what might strike us as the jarring incommensurability of the line, "That thousands of sweepers Dick, Joe, Ned & Jack," in "The Chimney Sweeper" in *Songs of Innocence* really need not be as contradictory as it might seem at first glance. It's true that if we assume that Dick, Joe, Ned, and Jack are each discrete, self-contained individuals, it becomes difficult to account for their collapse into the "thousands" of other sweeps. But, on the other hand, it could also be the case that the "thousands" can lapse into a mere four names because not all that much is riding on the four names in the first place. So that the distinctness of Dick, Joe, Ned, and Jack, their claim to individuality, is made merely in passing: these four stand in for the "thousands" rather than as ends in themselves because they are part of a collective existence that far exceeds their own limited individuality.

Similarly, "I" in Blake's work all too readily slides into "you" or "we," precisely because the lines and contours of the individual self, as an individual self, were not all that interesting to Blake. A case in point is in "The Lamb" in *Songs of Innocence*. In response to the first stanza's various formulations of the question, to the lamb, "who made thee?" the second stanza replies, "Little Lamb I'll tell thee! / He is called by thy name, / For he calls himself a Lamb: / He is meek & he is mild, / He became a little child: / I a child & thou a lamb, / We are called by his name."[1] I, we, thou, he – these are all blurred and fungible forms of identity, not fixed units. I can become you and you can become me and we can become him. Especially in the case of "The Lamb," of course, it is possible to read in larger philosophical or religious terms (which we have already encountered in different but related contexts in the preceding chapters) what is at stake in this collapse of hard and fast distinctions, and we can see here a reference to our common belonging – our common immanent participation – in God.

Individuals in Blake's works are always moving beyond their status as individuals; if anything, a sense of self is little more than a barrier cutting us off from our connections to others, and ultimately to God. For if "God only Acts & Is, in existing beings or Men,"[2] if "every thing that lives is holy,"[3] then what binds you to me and all of us to each other is our common (and again, that term, *immanent*) unity in God. "For Mercy Pity

Peace and Love, / Is God our father dear: / And Mercy Pity Peace and Love, / Is Man his child and care," we read in "The Divine Image," also in *Songs of Innocence*.[4] We will return in a later chapter to Blake's understanding of this immanent conception of God (a God constituted from below rather than existing independently of us from on high; we might say a radical and demotic God rather than an arrogant, tyrannical, judgmental, and punishing one). But what I want to at least register in passing here is that individual forms of identity are not by any means sealed off from each other in Blake's work; "I" am never really alone as an isolated, autonomous, selfish agent, but am always bound up with others, just as those thousands of chimney sweepers are bound up with each other.

For Blake, the glue that binds me to others and in the process helps define who and what "I" am, is desire. Like Blake's references to the self, however, this is a very different understanding of the notion of desire than the one we are used to, which is why I want to devote a chapter to exploring it and its relationship to the questions of being and identity with which it is intimately bound up in Blake's work. For, as I pointed out at the beginning of this chapter, we usually understand desire as the expression of an individual self, and in particular a necessarily selfish wish for something absent or other: I desire this or that, or him or her, for example. According to this conventional understanding, there is an "I" that, first of all, exists, and *then* has desires; the self pre-exists the desires, in other words. What I want to suggest is that in the case of Blake's work what we are seeing is not a self that pre-exists his or her own desires, but rather a form of being that exists *in* the desires themselves. This of course involves an immanent understanding of being to match the immanent understanding of God: we do not exist independently of our affective relations with others, but *in* those relations; as they change, we change; as they grow, we grow. And, as they diminish, we diminish.

If we re-approach "The Garden of Love" (which I discussed at length in the previous chapter) from this vantage point, what we will see is that the priests in black gowns walking their rounds and binding with briars my joys and desires are not simply cutting off or restricting the desires that I, as a selfish or autonomous agent, have. By restricting my desires, they are cutting off and restricting my very capacity for being. Ironically, rather than mourning the restriction or loss of the selfish desires of the individual, the poem is actually doing almost the exact opposite: it is mourning the reduction *into* individuality and the self. What the priests are doing, in other words, is not interrupting my selfishness, but rather restricting me into a self in the first place – which is far worse.

Now, putting it this way, I may have overstretched my argument, or got ahead of myself, so what I want to do now is to slow down and build this argument up again more slowly. Hopefully by the end of the chapter when we will revisit these points what I just wrote won't seem quite so strange after all.

Let's begin anew, then, with another of the *Songs*, though what I have in mind here is actually a pair of *Songs*, one from *Innocence* and the other from *Experience*: the two "Nurse's Songs," among the most intricately linked pieces in all of Blake's work. Here is the one from *Innocence*:

> When the voices of children are heard on the green,
> And laughing is heard on the hill,
> My heart is at rest within my breast,
> And everything else is still
>
> Then come home my children, the sun is gone down
> And the dews of night arise
> Come come leave off play, and let us away
> Till the morning appears in the skies
>
> No no let us play, for it is yet day
> And we cannot go to sleep
> Besides in the sky, the little birds fly
> And the hills are all covered with sheep
>
> Well well go & play till the light fades away
> And then go home to bed
> The little ones leaped & shouted & laugh'd
> And all the hills echoed.

And here is the one from *Songs of Experience*:

> When the voices of children, are heard on the green
> And whisperings are in the dale:
> The days of my youth rise fresh in my mind,
> My face turns green and pale.
>
> Then come home my children, the sun is gone down
> And the dews of night arise
> Your spring & your day, are wasted in play
> And your winter and night in disguise.

As I said, the links between the two pieces are startlingly explicit, given the shared lines. The fact that the opening line is the same in both poems and that the second line in the first poem takes us to the hills (open surfaces) whereas its counterpart in the second poem takes us to the dales or valleys (hidden depths) has been read to support readings of the pair of plates that see in them the opposition between the openness and the repression of the desiring self. Thus the "Nurse's Song" of *Innocence* has been read as an expression of the narrator's youthful pleasure and desire, whereas the "Nurse's Song" of *Experience* is taken to be about the repression – hardened by age – of her desires. In the first one, selfish pleasure is allowed to continue; in the second, it is shut down and cut off.

As we have seen before in reading *Songs of Innocence and of Experience*, while there is nothing necessarily wrong with the first or most obvious reading of either Nurse's song, there are other and perhaps more fruitful ways of reading the plates, especially in juxtaposition with one another. For it is possible to read the opposition between the *Innocence* and *Experience* versions not so much as one between selfish desire and repression but rather as an opposition between two different forms of being.

One of the most striking things about the first version of the song is that it ends with a turning out and away from the self. Another, related, point is that the dialogue between the nurse and the children is itself open, free-flowing, and amorphous rather than carefully delineated. Finally, the children exist and respond as a collective. As Robert Essick suggests, the thread-the-needle game they are playing is one in which the individual self – and the limits imposed by self-consciousness – dissolve into a collective through the act of communal play.[5] The sense of collectivity here is sufficiently expansive that it also invokes and is connected with a more general life force: the birds, the sheep, indeed, the hills themselves as signifiers of expansive, joyous life, echoing back the little ones' leaping, shouting, and laughing. But actually all these points are bound up with one another, and the poem ends with an affirmation of an expansive form of being and life in which oppositions between internal and external forces (including selves and others or even humans and nature) are seen to break down as the uncontained energy of life and being exceeds the parameters of individual selves. There is no such opening out in the "Nurse's Song" of *Experience*, however. The children do not respond, they do not have a voice, and they lack that expansive, creative energy that ties them to communal play and life more generally in the *Innocence* version of the poem. The words begin and end in the contained enclosure – the self – of the nurse herself.

So another way of viewing the juxtaposition of the two Nurse's songs is to read them in terms of an opposition between an expansive, communal, joyous form of being and a closed, individualistic one. What is interesting about reading the juxtaposition this way is that it changes how we bring desire into the reading. Rather than seeing the two works juxtaposing desire and repression, we can see, in the first, desire being aligned with a collective, amorphous, expansive form of being, whereas in the second, individuality is characterized by radically diminished desire. Desire, in other words – or at least this kind of desire – is not only *not* an attribute of the self: it is an attribute of which the narrowly enclosed or confined self seems incapable on its own, in isolation.

This reading is reinforced by the visual components of the two plates (see Figures 3.1 and 3.2), and in particular by the difference in their respective depictions of children: as an energized collective dancing/playing circle in the first, and as two very clearly delineated and immobilized individual selves in the second: selves closely contained by and subordinated to the dominating figure of the nurse, and framed, seemingly trapped, by the gate or doorway. In visual terms, in other words, the two plates all the more clearly juxtapose not desire and repression but rather, on the one hand, expansive being – a form of being in which individual distinctions and enclosures yield to joyous convergence and sharing – and, on the other hand, the framed, limited being of the individual, closed self.

Indeed, the visual relationship between the two plates also – as it so often does – brings to mind other works by Blake addressing similar questions. In 1790–91, Joseph Johnson, the publisher for whom Blake frequently produced engravings to illustrate books, commissioned from Blake a set of illustrations to accompany a new edition of Mary Wollstonecraft's *Original Stories from Real Life; with Conversations, Calculated to Regulate the Affections, and Form the Mind to Truth and Goodness*, which Johnson had first published in 1788. By now it should not surprise us that Blake might find problematic all that calculation and regulation, especially of children's minds, and many, if not all, of the illustrations Blake produced for Wollstonecraft's book seem quite skeptical or critical of its argument. The visual components of the "Nurse's Song" of *Experience* can be productively aligned with two of the illustrations for *Original Stories* (see Figures 3.3 and 3.4), in which we see the nurse in that collection of stories, Mrs. Mason (the one doing all the calculating, regulating, and in general binding with briars), exerting control over the two children. Wollstonecraft's stories are aimed at getting children to regulate themselves, to accept the confines of their being as self-regulating individuals. We can see Blake's illustrations exploring the sense of confinement and restriction of being involved in such a sense of self, and in fact also the sense of resistance to such restriction, especially in the second of the two images here (Figure 3.4), in which we see one of the children looking back or away from the direction the nurse is leading them.

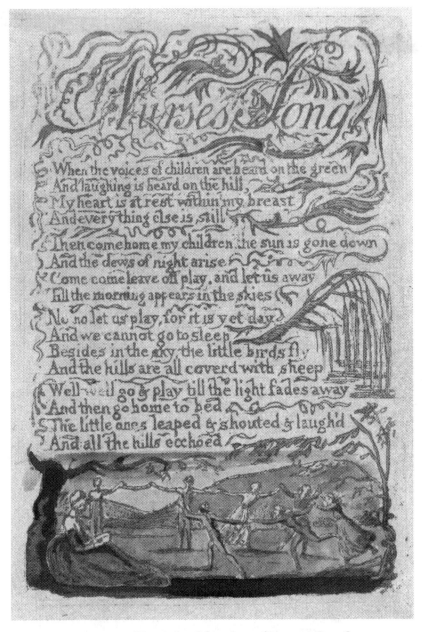

FIGURE 3.1. "Nurse's Song" from *Songs of Innocence*, Copy G.

> **NURSES Song**
>
> When the voices of children, are heard on the green
> And whisprings are in the dale:
> The days of my youth rise fresh in my mind,
> My face turns green and pale.
>
> Then come home my children, the sun is gone down
> And the dews of night arise
> Your spring & your day, are wasted in play
> And your winter and night in disguise.

FIGURE 3.2.   "Nurse's Song" from *Songs of Experience*, Copy L, plate 21.

Frontispiece.

*Look what a fine morning it is.—Insects,
Birds, & Animals, are all enjoying existence.*

Published by J. Johnson Sept.r 1.st 1791.

FIGURE 3.3.   "Look What a Fine Morning It Is," from Blake's illustrations for Mary
Wollstonecraft's *Original Stories from Real Life.*

Be calm, my child, remember that you must do all the good you can the present day.

Published by J. Johnson. Sept.ʳ 1. 1791.

FIGURE 3.4.   "Be Calm, My Child," from Blake's illustrations for Mary Wollstonecraft's *Original Stories from Real Life.*

FIGURE 3.5.   "Elohim Creating Adam."

Part of what all these images push us to think about, then, are the power relations involved in regulating and controlling the self, and binding with briars those desires that would take us beyond the self. Here we could turn to any number of other illustrations in Blake's work that explore the same relationship between power and the creation of the self, but the one that I have in mind (see Figure 3.5) is one of Blake's large colored prints dating from 1795, "Elohim Creating Adam." This colored print is important for our discussion because, while it recapitulates some of the visual language (primarily the outstretched arms of the powerful containing or enveloping the heads and bodies of the subordinated) that we can see in play in the "Nurse's Song" of *Experience* as well as Blake's illustrations to *Original Stories*, it also pushes in more expressly religious and biological directions. What is in those other works an act of *regulation* here appears in the guise of *creation* in both a religious sense (hence the divinity of the creating power) and a biological one (hence the fibrous, muscular, and sinewy depiction of the creating god – the image is two parts cosmic mystery mixed with three parts wormlike reproduction).

This convergence of a biological and cosmic or theological vocabulary with a social, educational, and institutional one can be one of the most confusing characteristics of Blake's work. What's potentially confusing is that without any apparent distinction, Blake can convey the regulation of the self (in, let's say, social terms – for example, in an educational setting, a school, a church) also as the creation of the self (in biological, cosmic, or theological terms). The act of framing the created, regulated, controlled self – which is to say, as far as Blake's works are concerned, the process of creating the self as a self in the first place – involves dynamics of power and submission. Thus the limited self, or individual selfhood, is not simply a site in which power is invested or contested: it is the product of power, and in particular of the power of social, religious, educational, and political institutions. This is what links the priests in black gowns of "The Garden of Love" to the nurse/teacher of "The Nurse's Song" or Blake's visual depictions of Mrs. Mason in Wollstonecraft's *Original Stories* and on to the creating divinity of "Elohim."

What can add to our confusion, if we are not careful, is the fact that creation in all of these senses or cases does not involve generation from out of nothing, but rather, much more specifically, a process of restricting what had been greater, possibly infinite, capacities, into more limited ones. Hence *binding* with briars our joys and desires, or, echoing the title of Wollstonecraft's book, *regulating* our affections, *forming* our minds to "truth and goodness." This a point worth repeating and emphasizing: this kind of creation is actually restriction – it involves a closing down, rather than an opening up, of possibilities. And that explains why in Blake's work the creation (of the self) is actually indistinguishable from confinement and regulation: he is using the cosmic, biological, or religious language of creation to push us to think through, to re-think, what we normally think of as social and historical processes.

The relationship between – or rather, the convergence of – the creation of an individual self and the regulation of that self is something that Blake explores at length in *The Book of Urizen*, *The Book of Ahania*, and *The Book of Los*. As we saw to a certain extent in the previous chapter, *The Book of Urizen* conveys Urizen's attempt to unilaterally impose his will on the world: to regulate the world, to bind it to the laws set forth in his book of bronze (Urizen's version of the Ten Commandments) by creating it, as though from out of nothing. This involves imposing order on hitherto unregulated life – "life in cataracts"[6] – and forcing it to take new shape in accordance with Urizen's will. Here too the language of framing or containing is indistinguishable from that of creating or

giving birth, and, moreover, the cosmic scale is rendered indistinguishable from that of the individual:

> And a roof, vast petrific around,
> On all sides He fram'd: like a womb;
> Where thousands of rivers in veins
> Of blood pour down the mountains to cool
> The eternal fires beating without
> From Eternals; & like a black globe
> View'd by sons of Eternity, standing
> On the shore of the infinite ocean
> Like a human heart strugling & beating
> The vast world of Urizen appear'd.[7]

Thus the creation of the limited, restricted world of Urizen – a whole
world also rendered on the scale of the individual human body – takes
place through the restriction or confinement of the infinite and eternal; or,
in other words, limited, finite forms are created not from out of thin air
but rather by imposing limits on what already exists. That is why I said
earlier that *restriction* into the self and the *creation* of the self as a self are,
for Blake, one and the same thing.

And the same goes for Urizen himself: just as he seeks to impose his will
on the world by restricting it and cutting it off from the infinite, he is also
formed in turn by Los. Los seeks to "imbody" or contain Urizen by
transforming disorganized elements and body parts into the body of
Urizen, first by "inclosing" Urizen's "fountain of thought," or in other
words his brain, then by working his way through all the other major body
parts and organs, described step by step in Blake's book. Once he is
"imbodied," Urizen becomes oblivious to the "myriads of Eternity: / All
the wisdom & joy of life," which "Roll like a sea around him, / Except
what his little orbs / Of sight by degrees unfold." Thus "his eternal life /
Like a dream was obliterated."[8] Once again, creation into a regulated self
involves a cutting off from the infinite and the eternal. We might think of
this as Blake's version of the fall.

What is at stake in conflating a biological language with a social or
institutional one is clearest, perhaps, in Blake's depiction of the formation
(again, the creation/restriction) of the inhabitants of the world of Urizen.
Like their master, they too are created in new forms – inhabiting new
bodies, new selves – by being cut off from the infinite. Thus they gradually
find themselves "bound down / To earth by their narrowing perceptions,"
unable to "rise at will / In the infinite void."[9]

Then – and this is the key here – they "form'd laws of prudence, and call'd them / The eternal laws of God."[10] Or in other words, they come to account for the process by which their lives, their forms of being, had been restricted, by ascribing it to divine intervention, and, in particular, to the laws of a God who had created them.

So let's sum up where we are in this argument. One of the recurring themes in Blake's work concerns the struggle to impose a certain kind of order on human life, and, for that matter, on all life. This is a struggle in which powerful forces (a certain kind of God, Urizen, Elohim) and/or their agents (priests, kings, nurses, teachers, beadles, parents) are deployed against the subordinated objects of their power (usually, especially in *Songs*, children). Insofar as it is successful, the process of binding and regulating our joys and desires (terms to which we will presently return at greater length, for we are not done with them yet) involves cutting us off from the eternal and the infinite and reducing us to individual, discrete selves, bound down to earth by our narrowing perceptions. This sense of restriction is tantamount to the creation of new forms of life, which – with what attenuated and limited senses yet remain to them – now perceive themselves and their world as inevitable and forever, inevitably, given: the products of the unanswerable dictates of God.

To this we need to introduce one more move in the line of thought developed by Blake. In conflating regulation and creation, he doesn't just link a biological language with a cosmic or theological one: he makes sure to also ground both in social, institutional, and historical processes tied directly to seventeenth- and eighteenth-century England. The key here is the persistent set of references in his work to perception, which we see at work in those passages I just quoted from *The Book of Urizen*. Similar references to the narrowing or restriction of our perceptions recur throughout Blake's work, from the earliest incarnations of the illuminated books (*All Religions Are One* and *There Is No Natural Religion*) all the way through the books of the 1790s and on to *Milton* and *Jerusalem*. More specifically still, we see throughout Blake's works references to the limitation of our perceptions to the five senses.

And it is in this extensive set of references to the five senses that Blake grounds his theological and biological language in social and historical circumstances. His work repeatedly insists that something happened to cut us off from the greater capacities of which we are still, in principle, capable – to cut us off from the infinite and the eternal and limit us only to the five senses of the individual body. "Man's perceptions are not bound by organs of perception," we read in *There Is No Natural Religion*; "he perceives more than sense (tho' ever so acute) can discover."[11] And yet, as we read in *The Marriage of Heaven and Hell*, "Man has closed himself up, till he sees all things thro' narrow chinks of his cavern."[12] These chinks in our cavern are the five senses to which our formerly infinite perceptions have now been restricted. "Five windows light the cavern'd Man," mocks the fairy at the beginning of *Europe*; "They told me that the night & day were all that I could see," laments Oothoon in *Visions of the Daughters of Albion*; "They told me that I had five senses to inclose me up; / And they inclos'd my infinite brain into a narrow circle."[13]

As for what it was that happened to cut us off from the infinite, that is the story told in *The Book of Urizen*, *The Book of Ahania*, and *The Book of Los*, among other places in the illuminated books. In *The Song of Los* we learn that social forces are involved in this restriction, and that "Churches: Hospitals: Castles: Palaces" are created "Like nets & gins & traps to catch the joys of Eternity," until "like a dream Eternity was obliterated & erased."[14] Here we have the same story again that we have seen in so many other places in Blake's work, but the references to social institutions helps ground us, and tie us to what we see at work for instance in "The Garden of Love" or the "Nurse's Song" of *Experience*. So does the continuing reference, a little later on the same plate of *The Song of Los*, to the Enlightenment, and most specifically to Bacon, Newton, and Locke, into whose hands, we read, Urizen gave "a Philosophy of Five Senses."[15]

Here is where things begin to fall a little more clearly into place, allowing us once and for all to tie the otherwise cosmic and biological to the social and historical. What Blake is pushing us to think about is the way in which at a certain moment in English history – the seventeenth century, to be precise – there emerged a certain way of thinking about the self in relation to society and the larger world around us. This involved not only developing a philosophy of discrete individuality, but also social structures and institutions premised on the notion that we are, or ought to be, self-regulating, discrete, intermeasurable individuals, capable of self-government and of the principles of exchange in a free market.

These social structures, the cornerstones of Occidental modernity, took well over a century to develop and be institutionalized after they were first systematically theorized in the seventeenth century. But the philosophical principles underlying them – above all, the emphasis on discrete and intermeasurable individuality – were vital to much of the radical culture of Blake's time, in the 1790s and after. This sought to challenge the logic of hereditary rule and aristocratic government on the basis of the notion of a universal set of rights shared by all men (and, some were already arguing, women as well) as rational, virtuous, self-governing, self-regulating individuals.

It should not come as a coincidence that these ideas should sound familiar from points raised earlier in this chapter, especially via our reading of "The Garden of Love" and the "Nurse's Song." For, notwithstanding Blake's sympathy with the radical opposition to hereditary rule and aristocratic government and various other forms of monopoly (political, economic, cultural, educational), he found deeply problematic and objectionable the idea that all we are reduced to is merely an interchangeable bunch of discrete self-regulating individuals. There seemed to him to be far more at stake in life than merely the right to control ourselves, the right to bind our own joys and desires, regulate our affections, form our minds to "truth and goodness," rather than being bound, regulated, and formed from the outside by "God & his Priest and King / Who make up a heaven of our misery."[16]

This brings us back to the question of perception and the business of the five senses. As ought to be clear by now, any form of restriction is a bad thing for Blake. Confinement into a limited, finite self, "barr'd and petrify'd against the infinite,"[17] is no less a form of confinement than imprisonment or burial alive. We are capable of more than that. Let's go back to those lines from *There Is No Natural Religion*: "Man's perceptions are not bound by organs of perception, he perceives more than sense (tho' ever so acute) can discover."[18] It is impossible to accept that we should perceive only what filters through the "five windows" that light our miserable caverned existence. And hence it is impossible to accept "inclosure" and the idea that we should be "bound down / To earth by [our] narrowing perceptions," unable to "rise at will / In the infinite void," or to accept the idea that we exist only in the limited and "petrify'd" forms of life whose creation is explored in *Europe* and *The Book of Urizen*, among other places: the forms of life that exist only as the products of power.

But if we reject the notion of limited perception and the form of limited, confined being with which it is associated, what exactly is the alternative? What other kind of existence can we have? The answer to these questions is provided already in *There Is No Natural Religion*, and it's an answer that Blake would continue to work on and develop all the way through the rest of the illuminated books. "The bounded is loathed by its possessor," we read there; "the same dull round even of a univer[s]e would soon become a mill with complicated wheels."[19] We must reach beyond the bounds of perception – and, more than that, beyond the bounds of the limited and caverned forms of life to which we have been condemned by social forces and processes since the seventeenth century. For, "the desire of Man being Infinite," we read, "the possession is Infinite & himself Infinite."[20]

In order to understand what it means to be infinite, we have to go back to the question of desire, which I raised at the beginning of this chapter. I warned there that we should be careful not to assume that "desire" means in Blake what it has come to mean in our own time as a reference to individual and ultimately selfish drives. If, as I pointed out earlier, the conventional understanding of desire sees it as the expression of a pre-existing self, Blake's understanding of desire is very different: what we see in it is a form of being that exists *in* desire. So that, as he expresses this idea in those lines from *There Is No Natural Religion*, if we can understand our desires as being infinite, we can understand our being as infinite as well.

Blake is articulating here a notion of being very different from the idea of self-regulating individual selfhood – a notion of being that flourished widely in the seventeenth century, before gradually being eroded and shut down by the social and historical transformations associated with what we now call modernization, which began in that moment and carried on through the eighteenth century and on into Blake's own lifetime. We see a very similar understanding of being that is present, for example, in the work of the seventeenth-century philosopher Spinoza, for whom the question of being is not a matter of either/or (as captured in Hamlet's well-known dilemma "to be or not to be") but rather a matter of more or less.[21] For Spinoza, in other words, we are capable of more being and less being, quite literally of being more or being less. That is because for Spinoza, we exist not as pre-determined forms or as organisms endowed with a certain limited capacity for perception; rather, we exist in our desires – our emotional bonds, our affective connections to others. The less extensive those are, the less being we have. The more extensive those ties and bonds, the more existence we have; the more our desires flourish, the more we exist. And the ultimate horizon of our existence is God, understood as the unity of all humanity or all life; for there is no other God.

If all this sounds somewhat familiar to us as students of Blake, it's because much the same approach to desire and being, equally rooted in the seventeenth century, is at stake in Blake's work. To accept the limited existence of the "caverned man," barred and petrified against the infinite, is to accept a radically curtailed and diminished form of being; to aspire to freedom from the cavern and a life of the imagination that takes us beyond the five senses is to reach out for a much greater – and ultimately infinite – form of being, one in which we can see ourselves caught up with each other and ultimately with "God himself," the "divine body" of which "we are his members."[22] The key here is Blake's notion of desire, in whose infinitude we can see the infinitude of our own being. For if we exist in our desires, rather than separately from them, desire marks the limits of our being; to limit it is to limit our existence; to cut it off is to cut off our being. As I said in the reading of "The Garden of Love" with which I opened this chapter, the priests in black gowns walking their rounds and binding with briars my joys and desires are not – as a conventional understanding of desire might have it – restricting the desires that I as a selfish agent have; by restricting my desires, they are cutting off and restricting my very capacity for being.

The limited and caverned form of being appropriate to self-regulating individual selves was not of much interest to Blake, for whom we exist not as replicable and intermeasurable units, but rather in our infinite desire to reach beyond ourselves, to see and to touch and participate in the infinite. Both philosophically and politically, this took Blake in a very different direction from the one articulated by most (but not all) of the radicals of his era, with whom he shared a common foe in the oppressive hereditary culture and politics of the established elite. Instead of a narrow Occidentalist discourse of self-governing rights, what he was interested in were the aesthetic and political possibilities opened up in the idea of thinking of life in terms of an infinite capacity for imagining and making, re-imagining and re-making; a capacity to which he referred as joy, to which we turn in the next chapter.

CHAPTER 4

Joy

It is clear enough, as we saw in Chapter 2, that there is something dangerously villainous about those priests in black gowns walking their rounds and binding with briars my joys and desires in "The Garden of Love." But it is worth asking what the opposite of such binding would amount to. What would the *flourishing* of desire look like? What I want to suggest in this chapter is that we can understand joy, in Blake's work, as just such a flourishing. In order for us to appreciate the significance of this, however, we have to bear in mind what desire means in Blake's work, and to recall the important differences – covered in Chapter 3 – between what has become the conventional understanding of desire (tending toward the selfish and the possessive) and the more unusual meaning of desire that we see at play in Blake's work.

For what we saw in the previous chapter is that in Blake's work desire is tied up with being: the more bound and restricted my desires, the less being I have; whereas the more expansive my desires and my connections to others, the more I exist – ultimately as a common participant in God, the "Divine Body," as Blake put it, of which "we are his members."[1] The question of the expansion and contraction of being is vital here because it reminds us that being in Blake is, or, rather (provided we can escape the clutches of Urizen, nurses, teachers, priests, and so on), it *ought* to be, open-ended, rather than fixed and solitary, contained within and defined by one single constant form. We might say that we exist in, and as, a cluster of relations, a network: the more the elements of that network, and the greater their variety, the more being we have. What is at stake here, then, is the ability to flourish by endlessly changing, shifting, and connecting with others; to be *both* the same *and* different as we change; indeed, to maintain a sense of unity with – rather than at the expense of – difference.

We can see this combination of unity and difference at work in Blake's understanding of God. "And all must love the human form, / In heathen, turk or jew. / Where Mercy Love & Pity dwell, / There God is dwelling too," we read in "The Divine Image" in *Songs of Innocence*. This immanent understanding of God does not impose unity at the expense of difference. We recognize the same God in the multiple and heterogeneous modes in which he appears – *with*, not *despite*, their various differences and distinctions. In other words, recognizing the fellow divinity of other human beings does not depend on seeing them as identical to us. For example, it is not insofar as they are Christians – or potential converts to Christianity – that we can recognize their fellowship with us (as, say, evangelicals in the late eighteenth century would have argued the point, seeing the other as really just a would-be self, "one of us"). Rather, it is in their very difference – as Muslims, Jews, heathens, and so on – that we can see that they are the same as "us." And hence we can see that "we" are united with, and in, our differences. Quite apart from any other consideration, this is a remarkably capacious understanding of racial difference for an Englishman writing as Britain's imperial project was shifting into high gear.

More than religious faith is at stake here, however. We could turn to the language of philosophy or critical theory to provide answers to the question of what it can mean to be the same while also always changing or being different. The seventeenth-century philosopher Spinoza, for example, elaborated a distinction between what he called the substance and modes of God: the substance of God is constant, but immanently composed by, and present in, an infinite variety of modes.[2] The twentieth-century French philosopher Henri Bergson, drawing on Spinoza, distinguished what he called the virtual and the actual in similar terms, arguing that a universal virtuality can be manifested in a variety of actual forms, just as the one universal God of Blake's "Divine Image," or, similarly, what Blake called Poetic Genius, exists in a variety of different, culturally and racially specific, forms.[3]

Bergson and Spinoza are immensely helpful in thinking through Blake at a conceptual level. But we need not rely on theological or philosophical conceptualizations to guide us here, for in thinking through the relationship of sameness and difference in Blake, we could just as easily turn back to the material dimension of Blake's work, which we addressed in the first chapter. In reminding ourselves that each of the illuminated books does not constitute a closed self-contained form whose being is defined once and for all but rather exists in a shifting range of multiple non-identical copies; and, moreover, in recalling that the entire corpus of the illuminated books exists as a network of shared, reiterated elements (including recycled images, concepts, even whole lines of text), many of which also spill over into, or borrow from, Blake's commercial works, we can recognize that we have already seen what this combination of unity with difference looks like in practice. We might say, for example, using the language of Bergson, that *The Book of Urizen* has a virtual existence that is actualized in each of its various copies. So, on the one hand, it exists multiply rather than in a single, constant form; but on the other hand that very multiplicity does not preclude a unity of some kind: we can still speak of *The Book of Urizen*, rather than merely copy A, copy B, copy C, and so on.

What is key here, then, is this notion of a unity that is constituted in and through variety and differentiation rather than through a static form of identity (for "the same dull round even of a univer[s]e would soon become a mill with complicated wheels").[4] Thus the more changes, variations, derivations, alterations each element of such a network has – the more it flourishes, in other words – the more being it could also be said to have, without, on the other hand, losing its coherence. Blake's illuminated books themselves offer perhaps the most profound illustration of such a flourishing. As I put it in the first chapter, we might say that Blake's works are characterized by a high degree of entropy: there are many ways that an illuminated book's constituent elements can be arranged and re-arranged without subverting the overall structure of the book (a feature demonstrated materially by the many variations and changes from copy to copy of *Songs*, *Urizen*, *America*, and so on). Whereas, as I suggested earlier, another kind of book, like a novel, has low entropy, in that even minor re-arrangements of its constituent elements would cause the overall structure to collapse in disorder.

Let's keep in our minds for now – and hopefully this will gradually come to make more sense – the possibility that the material form and function of Blake's work embodies or expresses his understanding of our very being. If we want to carry on with the language of physics, then, we might say that Blake's notion of our being involves the same high-entropy logic exhibited by his books. My being is not contained in a single low-entropy form or structure like a discrete, unique, self-contained selfhood, the slightest re-arrangement of whose constituent elements would cause its overall structure to collapse in incoherence, but rather in an endlessly changing, dynamic force field of desires, for which stasis, confinement, restriction, or binding would be tantamount to a slow and asphyxiating death. So if we exist as ever-changing bundles of relations articulated by our desires, rather than as fixed, rights-endowed, interchangeable units (individual selves in the narrowest and most conventional sense, including the one advocated by most of the radicals of Blake's day), *being more* involves an infinite pursuit of the desires defining us, a constant reaching out beyond the confines and limits of the conventional notion of the self.

Joy, we might say – "joy without ceasing"[5] – is the pursuit of being in precisely this sense, an expansive flourishing of being and desire. "How can a bird that is born for joy, / Sit in a cage and sing," asks the School Boy in *Songs of Experience*.[6] For joy as ceaseless energy, driven by our expansive desires, is incompatible with restriction of any kind, above all restriction into the solitary enclosed self.

In order to develop these ideas further, I want now to turn to "Laughing Song," in *Songs of Innocence*:

> When the green woods laugh with the voice of joy
> And the dimpling stream runs laughing by,
> When the air does laugh with our merry wit,
> And the green hill laughs with the noise of it.
>
> When the meadows laugh with lively green
> And the grasshopper laughs in the merry scene,
> When Mary and Susan and Emily.
> With their sweet round mouths sing Ha, Ha, He.
>
> When the painted birds laugh in the shade
> Where our table with cherries and nuts is spread
> Come live & be merry and join with me,
> To sing the sweet chorus of Ha, Ha, He.

The temptation here – taken up by many readings of this work – is to see the poem in conventional Romantic pastoral terms, as a celebration of the bounty and beauty of nature. Certainly the natural elements and themes are suggestive of a typically pastoral scene, in which the landscape beautifully and soothingly frames the human or social situation. It's all too easy to imagine Blake himself escaping the confines of London to bask in such a natural scene. At the time he wrote "Laughing Song," after all, he and Catherine were living in Poland Street, in the middle of gritty urban Soho. It would have been a matter of a few minutes' walk to the north for them to reach what is today the Euston Road or the Marylebone Road and cross the line from the urban into what were in the late 1790s the open fields lying just to the north of the metropolis and on toward Hampstead. Read in this way, "Laughing Song" seeks solace in the bosom of nature, and relief from the hectic pressures of urban life. It can be seen as stereotypically Romantic, charting the same kind of escape from social and urban pressures – the stress of life "In the great city, pent 'mid cloisters dim"[7] – and into Nature that one sees in the work of, say, Coleridge or Wordsworth: "sensations sweet, / Felt in the blood, and felt along the heart, / And passing even into my purer mind / With tranquil restoration."[8]

As tempting as such a reading may be, it doesn't allow for several key considerations. First, unlike either Coleridge or Wordsworth, Blake was an urban poet through and through. He spent his entire life in London other than three years of quasi-withdrawal under the auspices (and patronage) of the well-known poet William Hayley in Felpham on the south coast, which he finally abandoned, to return to London. No doubt Blake enjoyed a domestic garden, or the occasional walk into the countryside, as much as the next man, but London – that "Human awful wonder of God"[9] – remained very much at the heart of his life and work and there is no sign that he sought solace from it.

Moreover, and probably more important, Blake consistently expressed a distaste for Nature as such; that is, nature as something imagined to be separate from the human or the social. "Where man is not," as one of the proverbs of Hell in *The Marriage of Heaven and Hell* has it, "nature is barren."[10] Stemming from this was Blake's hostility to the idea of what he called the "Natural Man," the kind of man who, precisely like Wordsworth, seeks to ground his vision in Nature rather than the human and ultimately the social imagination. "Natural Objects always did & now do Weaken deaden & obliterate Imagination in Me," Blake complained about Wordsworth himself; "I see in Wordsworth the Natural Man rising up against the Spiritual Man Continually & then he is No Poet but a Heathen Philosopher at Enmity against all true Poetry or Inspiration."[11]

These lines help us see what is really at stake in "Laughing Song," which, for all its invocations of natural imagery, is a profoundly social poem. Indeed, its status as such is partly conveyed by the visual language of the plate, which recapitulates an earlier piece that Blake designed to illustrate drinking songs – those most social forms of poetry – in the 1783 edition of Joseph Ritson's *Select Collection of English Songs*. In this context we can think of the social as involving a crossing out of the narrow boundaries of limited selfhood.

For part of what is at stake in the poem is overcoming the distinction between self and other. This distinction was vital to what has come to be understood as the predominant Romantic differentiation of the human from the natural, or – to use the period's own terms – Man and Nature. Much of Wordsworth's poetry involves an attempt (or at least a claim) to reconnect Man to Nature, just as we see happening in "Tintern Abbey." But of course such a project – leaving aside the question of its sincerity – takes as its point of departure the idea that we are separate from nature to begin with, or that we have fallen into such a state of separation, so that I can imagine myself looking out over a natural object-world that is other to me.

For Blake, insofar as "everything that lives is holy," there is no such separation, any more than there is a separation between the human and the divine (or, again in the period's own terms, Man and God). Furthermore, just as the distinction between self and other is key to imagining an opposition between Man and Nature, it is also essential to the very logic of possessive individualism that Blake steadfastly opposed. For the idea of a self as opposed to others is built into the conception of independent, autonomous, self-regulating selfhood, with its careful and jealous policing of the very line between where "I" end and "you" begin (and by extension where my property ends and yours begins).

"Laughing Song" seeks to overcome all these polarizations and forms of opposition. What it offers instead is a profound unity, a sense of commonality and unruptured mutuality linking us all joyously together. And of course that is the point. If the commonality and mutuality – the extended sharing – celebrated by the poem is the essence of our being, joy expresses the flourishing of being under such open and unfettered circumstances. Thus, to say, as the poem's first line puts it, that "the green woods laugh with the voice of joy," is neither to anthropomorphize the woods nor merely to reduce them to an echo or a soundstage: the woods themselves, the stream, the birds, the air, the hill, are all constituent elements of an expansive form of being in which demarcations between self and other – including but not only the demarcation between Man and Nature – have no place. What we are left with instead is a sense of profound unity, a shared collective being that nevertheless also allows for an almost infinite variety of forms of differentiation and distinction. In other words, distinctness or difference is not only *not* the same thing as independent self-contained singleness: it is fully compatible with a shared underlying unity.

This combination of unity with difference is just what we saw in "The Divine Image," where the many variations and forms of distinction (heathen, Turk, Jew) are perfectly compatible with an underlying unity in the human form divine. Or, to return to the materiality of Blake's books, it is also what we see in the balance of, on the one hand, the marked distinctness of each copy of, say, *Songs of Innocence,* and, on the other hand, its participation in an underlying common being.

And so it goes also in "Laughing Song." The green woods, the air, the dimpling stream, the meadows, the grasshopper are all different expressions of the same underlying unity, as are also the different human figures. Thus Mary and Susan and Emily function here in much the same way as Dick, Joe, Ned, and Jack in "The Chimney Sweeper" of *Songs of Innocence*: they are not independent single characters but rather provisional forms of distinction still tapping into an underlying commonality.

This in turn explains the poem's extraordinary closing lines, "Come live & be merry and join with me, / To swing the sweet chorus of Ha, Ha, He." The sudden appearance of "me" here, and, with it, of the necessarily implied "you," seems to come from out of nowhere. It is as though the song is suddenly pushing us to ask, who am I, and who are you? Who are we in relation to each other? And in so doing we are taken back to the "I" and "thou" of "The Lamb" in *Songs of Innocence*, to a meditation on our being similar to the one occasioned by that song – and to a similar set of answers as well. You and I are bound up with each other, and with others in turn, and with all of life. To live is in this sense to be bound up with me and with others, and that in turn is to be merry: one of the terms (others include delight) associated in Blake's work with the state of joy. The joy conveyed by the song is the joy of being in this expansive sense, since the three states (living, joining, being merry) proposed by the first line of the last stanza are actually all variations on a single theme. Laughter, we might say, expresses the very joy of being.

Or, rather, laughter expresses the joy of being as freed from the prison of the five senses, which, as we saw in the previous chapter, confines us to a restricted sense of self, necessarily limited and cut off from the joyous state of being with others. For throughout Blake's work, access to or the denial of joy runs in parallel with the flourishing or the restriction of desire and of being more generally. To be merry, to be joyful, is to *be* – to have being – in the fullest sense, whereas a certain kind of mournfulness attends the situation of being bound or restricted, limited to the restrictive form of selfhood defined by the five senses. Thus joy in this particular sense demands of us the freedom to go beyond the limits of the ordinary regulated self, to escape the confines of the five senses.

This is a theme to which the illuminated books return over and again in different ways. "How do you know but ev'ry Bird that cuts the airy way, Is an immense world of delight, clos'd by your senses five?" asks one of the Devils in *The Marriage of Heaven & Hell*.[12] The point here is partly that the finite, confined, limited life within the trap of the self defined by the five senses cuts off and preempts other ways of seeing and imagining our being, and partly that those other more expansive ways of seeing and imagining our being involve delight, pleasure, and joy. This latter point is given particular emphasis in *The Marriage* by way of the connection it explicitly and consistently makes between joy and the form of printing that Blake used to produce the illuminated books – as though Blake's method of writing and printing, and the books produced as a result, have special access to the very form of joy they also represent.

This point is first registered explicitly in the passage that I just quoted from the mighty Devil in *The Marriage of Heaven & Hell*, and what is striking is that the passage, in the text itself, is written rather than spoken. To see the significance of this, it is worth contextualizing the passage more fully. It takes place in one of the Memorable Fancies that recur through the book. "As I was walking among the fires of hell, delighted with the enjoyments of Genius; which to Angels look like torment and insanity," explains the narrator, "I collected some of their Proverbs: thinking that as the sayings used in a nation, mark its character, so the Proverbs of Hell, shew the nature of Infernal wisdom better than any description of build-ings or garments. When I came home," he adds, "on the abyss of the five senses, where a flat sided steep frowns over the present world [,] I saw a mighty Devil folded in black clouds, hovering on the sides of the rock, with corroding fires he wrote the following sentence now percieved [*sic*] by the minds of men, & read by them on earth. How do you know but ev'ry Bird that cuts the airy way, Is an immense world of delight, clos'd by your senses five?"[13]

Although this passage represents Blake at his most playful, there is much at stake in it that goes beyond the immediate sense of cheekiness that it also undoubtedly conveys. Clearly, if "the following sentence" is now perceived by people and read by them on earth, that is so in the most literal and material sense because Blake himself printed it in *The Marriage* and we are now reading his book. Thus to have the mighty Devil *write* the line rather than *speak* it (there are plenty of speaking Devils elsewhere in the text) serves to emphasize the particular nature of Blake's own method of writing and printing books, and also the particular nature of reading that his books enables and sustains. Printing and reading in this method pushes – and indeed enables – us to go beyond the limits of conventional thought as well as conventional methods of printing and reading: it allows us to see, as though for the first time, those immense worlds of delight that would otherwise be invisible to us from the confines of the limited form of self structured by the five senses.

What should especially interest us in the context of the present chapter is that access to this more expansive way of thinking and seeing is also a matter of joy. It is no coincidence, in other words, that it is specifically an immense world of *delight* that we are being exhorted to imagine as we read Blake's books. This tying together of Blake's method of printing with delight, pleasure, and joy is a point to which *The Marriage* returns even more explicitly a few plates later, in another of the Memorable Fancies which it is also worth quoting at length because it draws together all of the themes I have been discussing so far in this chapter:

> The ancient tradition that the world will be consumed in fire at the end of six thousand years is true. as I have heard from Hell.
>
> For the cherub with his flaming sword is hereby commanded to leave his guard at the tree of life, and when he does, the whole creation will be consumed, and appear infinite. and holy whereas it now appears finite & corrupt.
>
> This will come to pass by an improvement of sensual enjoyment.
>
> But first the notion that man has a body distinct from his soul, is to be expunged; this I shall do, by printing in the infernal method, by corroding, which in Hell are salutary and medicinal, melting apparent surfaces away, and displaying the infinite which was hid.
>
> If the doors of perception were cleansed every thing would appear to man as it is: infinite.
>
> For man has closed himself up, till he sees all things thro' narrow chinks of his cavern.

What we have here is an explicit triangulation of the same three notions which we have been discussing all along, and which are in Blake's work clearly tied to one another. First is the idea that our quasi-voluntary restriction into individual selfhoods granting us access to the outside world only through the grid or the filter of the five senses – the doors of perception – cuts us off from the infinite. Second is the idea that joy, including sensual joy, involves breaking the limits of the five senses and escaping the confines of our "caverned" existence, in effect *using* the senses in order to overcome them. Third, recapturing the written statement of the mighty Devil in that earlier plate, is the idea that there is a direct relationship between joy in this expansive (or explosive) understanding of joy and Blake's method of printing.

As we saw in previous chapters, Blake's method works not by imposing (for example, by setting forth, stamping black ink on white paper), but rather the other way around, by erasing, burning, corrosives – revealing, among other things, the gaps and spaces *between* the words as much as the words and images themselves. The words and images are given shape from out of the background in which they are contained, rather than being imposed on that background – precisely as though they were there all along in virtual form (to use the language of Bergson), waiting to be actualized. A copper plate can thus be thought of as a surface through which we can access an infinite (virtual) potential, rather than simply as a finite and limited actual space on which ideas and images can be imposed. Certain ideas, lines, images can re-appear, be re-actualized, because they are still there, waiting to come out again – and to change and be changed in their very re-appearance. Even after being transferred to paper, this form of printing still maintains as much as possible of its potentiality, as the "same" print is altered through the very process of being repeated, and as the "same" book takes on one dazzling new form after another.

Here we can begin to tie up one of the interpretive threads we have been following through this chapter: rather than sustaining the blind repetition of inert, lifeless, constant, unchanging, interchangeable, identical prints, Blake's method of printing and the books produced as a result allow for change through repetition. The more something is repeated, the more it changes. Rather than standing still, it flourishes through repetition and change. But what does all this have to do with joy?

Joy, we might say, also involves the melting away of such apparent surfaces – not only the surface of the plate or the text, but also other kinds of surfaces, ones that seem to separate inside from outside, closed from open, finite from infinite, and self from other. Or in other words, joy involves escaping confines, restrictions, and limitations and flourishing beyond their limits, and changing through repeated interaction with others. Blake's idea of a book thus needs to be seen in relation to modes of interaction – including physical interaction and pleasure – that similarly defy reduction into the enclosed self by enabling a connection, whether corporeal or spiritual or otherwise, beyond its limits. To experience such joy is to find life beyond the self, to touch the infinite.

"Come live & be merry and join with me, / To sing the sweet chorus of Ha, Ha, He." We have indeed already seen one way of thinking of this, in "Laughing Song," but Blake's fullest meditation on the question of joy, or rather this triangulation of related questions in relation to joy, unfolds in one of his most ambitious works, *Visions of the Daughters of Albion*. The complexity of this work defies any easy encapsulation, so I am not going to attempt such a reductive or summarizing move here (such an attempt would take over the chapter) and will instead refer readers to the text itself and to the countless scholarly readings that aim to situate it in the various interpretive contexts in which it makes an intervention, including discussions of marriage, colonialism, transatlantic slavery, women's rights, and sexuality more generally.

I do, however, want to highlight the figure of Oothoon in *Visions of the Daughters*. We can think of her as a jilted or betrayed lover, a victim of patriarchal violence and of the bonds, whips, brands, and chains of slavery (and part of the point of the text, I think, is that it urges us to think of the relationships among and between these different domains). Most central to the treatment of Oothoon, however, is her refusal of the logic of entrapment, confinement, and regulation, and her insistence, insofar as it is possible for her to insist, on openness, freedom, and the flourishing enabled by variability and change – precisely the attributes we have seen identified with joy elsewhere in Blake's work.

"Open to joy and to delight where ever beauty appears,"[14] Oothoon is, we might say, the very embodiment of joy. But to see the significance of this we need to attend carefully to her treatment in the text. We need to understand her as rejecting the logic of confinement in the solitary self. "They told me that the night & day were all that I could see," she laments; "They told me that I had five senses to inclose me up. / And they inclos'd my infinite brain into a narrow circle, / And sunk my heart into the Abyss, a red round globe hot burning / Till all from life I was obliterated and erased."[15] These are by now familiar themes and we have seen them in play elsewhere in Blake's work, including the passages from *The Marriage* which I quoted a little earlier, but also *The Book of Urizen* and other texts. Here they recapitulate the opposition between an infinite life and the limited and confined life of the self "inclosed," as Oothoon puts it, in the "red round globe" defined by the five senses.

Oothoon, however, extends this opposition into a treatment of two different modes of sexual relationship and what goes under the banner of love. She refuses the conventional role of wife to which she would be condemned not merely by her erstwhile lover Theotormon but enveloping social forces. "Can that be Love, that drinks another as a sponge drinks water?" she asks. "That clouds with jealousy his nights, with weepings all the day: / To spin a web of age around him. grey and hoary! dark! / Till his eyes sicken at the fruit that hangs before his sight." Such, she adds, making the point explicit, "is self-love that envies all! a creeping skeleton / With lamplike eyes watching around the frozen marriage bed."[16] Oothoon also articulates an alternative to this vision of restriction, confinement, closure, and all but frosty death. "Love! Love! Love! happy happy Love! free as the mountain wind!" she cries. "Silken nets and traps of adamant will Oothoon spread, / And catch for thee girls of mild silver, or of furious gold; / I'll lie beside thee on a bank & view their wanton play / In lovely copulation bliss on bliss with Theotormon: / Red as the rosy morning, lustful as the first born beam, / Oothoon shall view his dear delight, nor e'er with jealous cloud / Come in the heaven of generous love; nor selfish blightings bring."[17] This passage has long been read as an articulation of a notion of free love rather than monogamy, and even more specifically as articulating a notion of free love for men, in which women are subservient, merely the playthings of male desire, or, worse, trapped by a sexual order that satisfies male desire at the expense of women. Oothoon, after all, offers to "catch" and "trap" other girls to satisfy Theotormon, to derive her own presumably limited form of sexual satisfaction by watching him obtain his own satisfaction by copulating with other women. Female desire can be seen here as subordinated and secondary to male desire.

No doubt the passage does make available such quasi-misogynistic readings (even if that is not the only way to think of the expression of female desire in *Visions of the Daughters*). But although the narrowly sexual dynamics of the text are important here, the passage also pushes us to think in terms of domains other than that of sexuality.

For one thing, the contrast between the "frozen marriage bed" and love "free as the mountain wind" involves more than merely sexual politics: it also hinges on the contrast that recurs throughout Blake's work between the fixed (limited, confined, trapped, "inclosed") and the variable (free, changing, flourishing). Moreover, embedded in this contrast is a connection to two different modes of reproduction, which is implicitly tied here to sexual reproduction, but appears elsewhere in Blake's work in terms of other forms of reproduction, printing above all.

Indeed, the treatment of sexual reproduction in conventional marriage as sanctioned by state religion in *Visions of the Daughters* is also explicitly linked to other domains of power and authority. "With what sense does the parson claim the labour of the farmer?" asks Oothoon in one of the text's most remarkable passages. "What are his nets & gins & traps. & how does he surround him / With cold floods of abstraction, and with forests of solitude, / To build him castles and high spires. where kings & priests may dwell. / Till she who burns with youth. and knows no fixed lot; is bound / In spells of law to one she loaths: and must she drag the chain / Of life, in weary lust! must chilling murderous thoughts. obscure / The clear heaven of her eternal spring? to bear the wintry rage / Of a harsh terror driv'n to madness, bound to hold a rod / Over her shrinking shoulders all the day; & all the night / To turn the wheel of false desire: and longings that wake her womb / To the abhorred birth of cherubs in the human form / That live a pestilence & die a meteor & are no more."[18]

If, after all, "spells of law" bind a woman to a man in conventional state-sanctioned marriage, it should come as no surprise that there are ties between the institution of marriage (in this form at any rate) and the wider structures of power, authority, and the exploitation of labor, just as we see "the marriage hearse"[19] connected to the institutions of commerce, state religion, and state power in "London" in *Songs of Experience*. Sexual reproduction that takes place in the "frozen marriage bed" is just another form of labor, just as entrapping, just as exploitative, as other forms of exploitation that sustain the wider economy of extraction and abuse of power that is ruled over by kings and priests in their castles and high spires. Such a form of reproduction is merely replicative, a kind of drudgery that is directly equivalent – and indeed directly tied by the passage – to the grinding tedium of factory labor, that produces a stream of identical, fixed, static, closed, interchangeable products.

This then ought to prompt a further consideration of the logic of free love advocated by Oothoon as an alternative to the selfish love of conventional marriage as sanctioned by the state and its institutions. It is not just a matter of sexual pleasure in the narrowest sense but can be seen also as the key to an entirely different economy of power and production. The selfish economy of power ruled over by kings and priests is predicated to the exploitative reproduction of sameness, identity, interchangeable commodities, and indeed selves or subjects. The alternative being articulated by Oothoon is tied to a very different mode of production and an entirely different order of existence, open rather than closed, variable, and changing rather than static, and above all premised on an ever-shifting set of connections to others – "copulation" not simply in the more limited sexual sense of that term, but in the more general sense of a linking and connecting together.

Hence the connection to joy as a form of linking together and flourishing through variety and change. Oothoon repeatedly makes this connection explicit, as when she confronts Urizen and challenges the false and reductive form of joy, the one kind of joy that he would impose on the world with his unilateral dictation ("One command, one joy, one desire / One curse, one weight, one measure / One King, one God, one Law").[20] "O Urizen!" she cries, "Creator of men! Mistaken Demon of heaven: / Thy joys are tears! thy labour vain, to form men to thine image. / How can one joy absorb another? are not different joys / Holy, eternal, infinite! and each joy is a Love."[21] The labor that aims to reproduce singularity – copying the one same image over and again – is tied here to an attempt to enclose and restrict joy itself, to restrict joy to singularity. For Oothoon, however, the point of joy is that it refuses that reduction just as much as she herself refuses confinement into the prison of the five senses into which "they told me" we have to be "inclosed." The forms of joy and of love to which Oothoon commits herself, by contrast, are premised on sharing, connection, mutuality, and indeed to the infinite; to a logic of unity tied to, rather than at odds with, endless variability, change, and difference; to a flourishing of desire – and of being itself, being in connection with others.

There is no doubt that to our modern eyes and ears connecting the politics of joy to sexuality in the way in which Oothoon does so in *Visions of the Daughters of Albion* can sound and look, at best, clumsy and naïve, if not altogether (or at least potentially) misogynistic. But *Visions of the Daughters* is not the only text in which Blake brings together and connects his critique of the selfish existence trapped within the paradigm of the five senses to a liberating discourse of joy. Perhaps his most explicitly "political" work, *America*, makes precisely the same connection, in its affirmation of "the fiery joy that Urizen perverted to ten commands,"[22] and its vision of political liberation tied to the erasure of the limits imposed by selfish existence, as we see, in its closing lines, "the five gates"[23] consumed and destroyed in the flames of revolution, "their bolts & hinges melted"[24] in the announcement of a new political, and affective, order. To connect Blake's understanding of joy to the political struggles unfolding in his lifetime, however, will require another chapter.

CHAPTER 5

Power

I want to begin this discussion of the question of power in Blake's work by reading the two "Chimney Sweeper" plates from *Songs of Innocence and of Experience* in relationship to one another. What we will find in the juxtaposition of the two "Chimney Sweeper" texts is an invitation to think through the question of the relationship of power to narrative and textuality, and, through that, the larger question of social power and how one can start imagining possibilities of resistance to it. What I propose in this chapter is that Blake, in his work, pushes us to think through how power operates on a variety of different – and yet interlocking or overlapping – scales. And hence his work also prompts us to question how power can be contested or resisted all along those different scales. Part of what is at stake here is how we understand the role of reading and interpretation in either the distribution or the containment of power. Although power can of course operate through brute strength, it is generally far more efficient, and can be invisible or inscrutable, when it operates more subtly, for instance, by helping to form our thoughts or define the contours of our interpretive universe, filling in, as it were, the blanks of our own thoughts even as we are in the process of thinking them.

Let's turn to the "Chimney Sweeper" of *Songs of Innocence* first to see Blake's approach to the question of power.

> When my mother died I was very young,
> And my father sold me while yet my tongue,
> Could scarcely cry weep weep weep weep.
> So your chimneys I sweep & in soot I sleep.
>
> There's little Tom Dacre, who cried when his head
> That curl'd like a lambs back was shav'd, so I said,
> Hush Tom never mind it, for when your head's bare,
> You know that the soot cannot spoil your white hair.

And so he was quiet, & that very night,
As Tom was a sleeping he had such a sight,
That thousands of sweepers Dick, Joe, Ned & Jack
Were all of them lock'd up in coffins of black,

And by came an Angel who had a bright key,
And he open'd the coffins & set them all free.
Then down a green plain leaping laughing they run
And wash in a river and shine in the Sun.

Then naked & white, all their bags left behind,
They rise upon clouds, and sport in the wind.
And the Angel told Tom, if he'd be a good boy,
He'd have God for his father & never want joy.

And so Tom awoke and we rose in the dark
And got with our bags & our brushes to work.
Tho' the morning was cold, Tom was happy & warm.
So if all do their duty, they need not fear harm.

It is so easy, so tempting, so obvious, to read the final stanza or two as confirming what has been consolidated and conveyed to us as the traditional mainstream Protestant view that our reward for suffering in this life will be in the happy expectations of the life in the hereafter. The immediate temptation, in other words, is to read the words of the poem in a strictly conventional sense as affirming the idea that all of the children's suffering can be justified by the offer of having God for a father; that they can accept bodily harm (like that inflicted by sweeping chimneys and living encrusted in carcinogenic soot) in the here and now by being supposedly relieved of harm in a deferred future. Indeed it is made quite explicit in the poem that the children can go on with their work precisely because of this hope and expectation. "Duty" is made possible by a removal of fear – and just so do the little brutalized children get with their bags and brushes back to work.

To the attentive Blakean, of course, alarm bells ought to be going off by now. Duty and the grueling exploitation of child labor is not a value we often see endorsed in Blake's work. When duty does come up elsewhere in Blake it is enunciated or demanded by slavers like Bromion (in *Visions of the Daughters of Albion*) or taskmasters like Urizen, who after all demands loyalty and obedience – the fulfillment of duty and expectations – from his children. Duty is something associated in Blake's work with war and destruction, a dystopian condition in which we can imagine that "all Love is lost," as we read in *Jerusalem*, and that "terror succeeds & Hatred instead

of Love / And stern demands of Right & Duty instead of Liberty."¹ So
the endorsement of the filial logic of duty that we see at the end of
"Chimney Sweeper" should be cause for concern rather than the easy
satisfaction or complacency with which we might associate it if we let
our guard down and think of Blake as a conventional writer espousing
the conservative ideas of, say, the eighteenth-century evangelical crusader
Hannah More.

There are other danger signs here as well, precisely in the relationship
between duty and filial relationships. What is offered through the device of
the vision superintended by the Angel is a new father figure, a new kind of
parent. But what sense do we get of parents as figures of authority in the
text? The child's mother has, in effect (at least from a childish point of
view), betrayed him; his father has doubled that betrayal by selling him
into a life of servitude and (as was generally well known by the end of the
eighteenth century given the widespread humanitarian discussion of the
state and condition of chimney sweepers) almost inevitable crippling or
cancerous death. And what do the new or substitute authority or parental
figures – the Angel and his God – offer but the confirmation and consoli-
dation of that virtual death sentence? Here as elsewhere in Blake's work,
parental or authority figures in general – of whom Urizen is the ultimate
example – are far from trustworthy. They are generally out to trap, control,
regulate, or exploit us, to bind with briars our joys and desires.

There is so much more that one can add about this poem, including the
role of the relationship between the narrator ("I") or narrators ("we") and
Tom Dacre (for example, how do we shift from seeing Tom Dacre from
the outside to seeing the world from his point of view in Tom's vision of
the sweepers freed by the Angel?). For the purposes of our discussion here,
however, the most important move in the text is the one that unites, on
the one hand, what ought to by now be clear is the dangerously entrapping
narrative of future redemption as a justification for adhering to "duty" and
suffering in the present (a narrative presented via one of the authority
figures, the Angel); and, on the other hand, the conventional reading that,
unless we are on our guard, we ourselves half-consciously project on to the
text, taking up its invitation to fill in its ideological blanks. Thus there is a
trick that the text plays on us: it is only in retrospect, or on further
consideration (hang on, wait a minute: this is Blake, not Hannah More!)
that we realize that the narrative presented by these authority figures
is designed to enable the continuing brutalization and exploitation of
children – and that that enablement is in effect condoned by our own
careless reading of the text. It's careless in that we can embark on such a

reading only by losing sight of the consistent critique of authority figures and their narratives of power that runs all through Blake's work.

The point is that the "Chimney Sweeper" of *Innocence* is at its most effective when it forces us to look in the mirror and realize that we too are subject to such narratives of power, and that we too can be seduced and trapped by them, turn to them, wrap ourselves up in them, if we are not more careful. When this becomes clear, the text demands a second reading and a third and more beyond that, now carefully attuned to its many self-undermining ironies. This is a text, in short, that all but begs for ironic and subversive readings.

In this sense, "The Chimney Sweeper" of *Songs of Experience* makes for an altogether different reading:

> A little black thing among the snow:
> Crying weep, weep in notes of woe!
> Where are thy father & mother? say?
> They are both gone up to the church to pray.
>
> Because I was happy upon the heath,
> And smil'd among the winters snow:
> They clothed me in the clothes of death.
> And taught me to sing the notes of woe.
>
> And because I am happy, & dance & sing,
> They think they have done me no injury:
> And are gone to praise God & his priest & King
> Who make up a heaven of our misery.

This text too has its many temptations. The chimney sweeper here has nothing but contempt for the narrative of redemption through suffering and hard work that – his counterpart in *Songs of Innocence* seems to accept – guides us on the path to salvation. Unlike that counterpart too, he is acutely aware not only of the state and extent of his own brutalization and degradation but also, perhaps more importantly, of its relationship to wider structures of authority and power extending through the family and on to church and state. Indeed, he is aware that there is a direct, causal, and structural relationship between the behavior of the authority figures in his life – primarily his parents, but through them priest, king, and God as well – and his own exploitation and brutalization. It's worth pointing out, in fact, that the chimney sweeper is echoing, albeit in a corrosively critical way, Edmund Burke's contention that Britons bind up "the constitution of our country with our dearest domestic ties; adopting our fundamental laws into the bosom of our family affections; keeping inseparable and cherishing with the warmth of all their combined and mutually reflected charities our state, our hearths, our sepulchers, and our altars."[2] The same line between family affections, the state, and state religion is traced in Blake's poem, only this time in a distinctly critical way, allowing us, in effect, to see the state and other forms of authority as neglectful or downright abusive parents.

As with its counterpart in *Songs of Innocence*, there are, again, many more things to say about this text, but for the purposes of our immediate discussion two points are most important. First, the relationship between power and exploitation expressed by the young chimney sweeper is shown to be driven not merely by subservience to power but more specifically by faith in the textual narratives of power. His parents are praying, after all; that is, engaging in a textual relationship with the guarantors of order and power, if only by repeating what they are told by those higher up in the chain of authority (think here of the visual components of "The Garden of Love," Figure 2.1, discussed in Chapter 2). And, beyond that, the sweep is aware that the "made up" world invoked by such prayers is exactly what sustains "our misery." Unlike the parents of the "Chimney Sweeper" of *Innocence*, in other words, the parents here are not directly engaged in betraying their child – abandoning him or selling him, as in the other poem. Instead, they are more subtly complicit by participating in the textual structures of power; it is the praise they offer to God and priest and king that creates the made-up heaven sustaining the ongoing exploitation of their child and other children.

The second very important point to make here is that, for all his awareness, the chimney sweeper not only *was* happy before they clothed him in the "clothes of death," he is *still* happy, and dances and sings, even though he is manifestly aware of the injury he has sustained and will continue to sustain into an undetermined future. This very happiness raises the stakes for understanding the paths of resistance to power that always seem to operate alongside it in Blake's work. For even as he is also being prompted and guided to read one way and to "sing the notes of woe," the chimney sweeper is also capable of reading differently and singing alternatives to sustain happiness – joy – in the face of woe and misery. This suggests not merely a kind of resilience on his part, a capacity to endure exploitation, but also an investment in forms and currents of resistance to the logic of power, and even in forms of textuality, including songs, that defy power even if they don't ultimately succeed in overturning it.

We have already seen in previous chapters of this book the tension between different modes of textuality and interpretation in Blake's work.

Blake was interested in the differences between closed texts and open ones, or, in other words, texts that, on the one hand, try to channel and contain their own reading or interpretation by attempting to impose a structure around the act of reading itself (guidelines to which the reader ought to adhere in approaching the text, or keys to interpretation, filters and grids for reading, and so on); and, on the other hand, texts that actively encourage us to trace our own interpretive paths not merely through them but also perhaps beyond them, connecting them to a proliferating network of other texts. We see references to both kinds of texts in Blake's work, running the gamut from Urizen's books of iron to which all are commanded to pledge their (literally) blind allegiance, to the open and almost infinitely playful form of reading which Blake's own books encourage us to participate in as we move from one component to another and even start to see whole books as constituted by an ever-shifting network of visual and verbal components shared in common with other such networks.

Blake's books, as I suggested in Chapter 1, encourage us to think of the text we read not as permanent or independent of our reading but rather as located and actualized in the paths we ourselves trace as we join together these different components differently in successive readings. Thus their very openness enables a joyous sense of interpretive proliferation which we can recognize in the form of opposition it offers to hierarchically structured, ordered, contained forms and styles of reading more appropriate to very different (what we might tentatively, though not without good reason, call authoritarian) forms of power: texts that want to make us bow down and pray to them.

What we now need to do is to trace more completely the relationship between that authoritarian form of textuality and the structures of power more generally. For power, it turns out, depends directly on textual structures and codes, or rather on the attempt to cajole, betray, seduce, or coerce us into accepting its interpretive codes, its mind-forged manacles (as "London" in *Songs of Experience* portrays them).

This is exactly what we see in our first encounter with the "Chimney Sweeper" of *Songs of Innocence*, which sets us up to read the dream the Angel offers to Tom Dacre at face value, thereby accepting that we must all do our "duty" irrespective of the social and indeed bodily injury we sustain as a result. It's only when we go *back* and challenge that conventional wisdom that we acquire the kind of insight offered by the chimney sweeper of *Songs of Experience*; an insight that fundamentally requires re-reading as part of its practice. Blake engages with interpretive codes, like the one with which we are initially tempted to read the "Chimney Sweeper" of

Innocence, throughout the illuminated books. Moreover, we can also very usefully see such an engagement at play in his own readings of other texts and in the surviving annotations and marginal notes he made in those books, in which we witness a very methodical set of meditations on the relationship between textuality and authority or power more generally.

Blake's notes and annotations to Robert Thornton's 1827 translation of, and notes on, the Lord's prayer is particularly instructive in this regard. Part of what Thornton aimed to do in his politically as well as theologically conservative work – which Blake detested – was to contain the many radical interpretive possibilities opened up by other readings of the text of the Lord's prayer. Many of Blake's scribbled marginal comments are humorous (including the one where he notes that Thornton's revision of the Lord's prayer has turned it so back to front that we might as well be reading it backward, "which they say raises the Devil").[3] But most of his scribbles are concerned in one way or another with the distribution of power, and for that matter, wealth, or in other words, in textual terms, the tension between interpretations of the text (like Thornton's) intended to reinforce the power of the state and the established order as opposed to interpretations that open the text up to a vision of universal sharing and being in common.

Blake's text is concerned above all with the politics of interpretation. Thornton opens with a passage from Dr. Johnson asserting that the Bible "is the most difficult book in the world to comprehend, nor can it be understood at all by the unlearned, except through the aid of CRITICAL and EXPLANATORY notes."[4] To this, Blake – espousing the cause of the unlearned – fires back that "Christ & his Apostles were Illiterate Men," whereas "Caiphas Pilate & Herod were Learned." He adds that "the Beauty of the Bible is that the most Ignorant & Simple Minds Understand it Best."[5] Blake is here saying something more complex than merely that there are competing readings of the Bible; those readings are explicitly aligned with the interests of those in power or else in opposition to those interests, as seen from the standpoint of the unlearned, the despised, and the marginalized (chimney sweepers not unnaturally come to mind in this context).

What is at stake here has to do with power, in other words, rather than merely a kind of variability of interpretation, or rather a struggle over the interpretation of texts and indeed the world around us. Blake identifies Thornton with the learned, of course, and specifically with what he calls "the classical learned" and their "most Malignant and Artful attack" on the unlearned.[6] This attack involves the attempt to impose a moral code, or in other words to define a politics of morality that would structure our actions through dictation ("Thou shalt not," as the door over the chapel in "The Garden of Love" puts it). The "CRITICAL and EXPLANA-TORY notes" with which "the learned" approach a text can be seen as serving as a kind of corollary for their wider attitude toward moral codes more generally; that is, a grid or filter to structure or guide interpretation and the energy of life.

This is quite radically at odds with the approach taken by "the unlearned," and above all by Jesus, who from this standpoint can be seen as the very embodiment of the unlearned (and one can readily see here the influence of antinomian thought on Blake, to which I have referred in previous chapters). For, far from needing critical or explanatory notes, Jesus, Blake writes, "supposes every Thing to be Evident to the Child & to the Poor & Unlearned." Such, he adds, "is the Gospel."[7] For, he adds, "the Whole Bible is filld with Imaginations & Visions from End to End & not with Moral virtues that is the baseness of Plato & the Greeks & all Warriors." The "Moral Virtues," Blake explains, "are continual Accusers of Sin & promote Eternal Wars & Domineering over others."[8] We return in a later chapter to a fuller discussion of Blake's notion of the imagination, but for now it's worth at least noting that the contrast between imagination and vision, on the one hand, and the warrior logic of moral codes on the other, is directly related to the opposition running throughout Blake's work between desire and regulation.

That is to say, there is a relationship between modes of reading and of being in Blake's work; a correlation between how we interact with texts (and how they interact with or seek to control us) and how we live. To read with imagination and vision, to read openly and creatively, is to articulate a mode of reading (and hence of textuality more generally) appropriate to the joyous, expansive mode of being and desire celebrated in Blake's work, which we have discussed at length in the preceding chapters of this book. Whereas to read in the warrior mode and in the service of moral logic and moral codes and in the name of moral virtue is to read in a restricted, regulated, confined way, the limitation of the kind of reading directly correlating with the limited form of being to which it corresponds. In other words, the moral codes of warrior culture – the culture that "the learned" seek to impose on us – involve an attempt to regulate, limit, and contain our very being, and not merely how we read or interact with texts. Thus it is no coincidence that the "Thou shalt not" writ over the door in "The Garden of Love" is a mode of textuality associated with the priests walking their rounds and binding with briars our joys and desires and hence our being: these logics work coextensively, reinforcing each other. To command us in writing (and hence in our reading of what is written) is to command, or at least it expresses the will to command, our desire and hence our being itself.

We can see this link in the critique of the five senses that runs continually throughout Blake's work. Our restriction into limited units of being "barr'd and petrify'd against the infinite" is made possible by – it is inseparable from – the process that limits and restricts how we read the world around us. Thus to see the world only through what we can now recognize as the interpretive grid imposed by the five senses, the "five windows" that "light the cavern'd Man," not only cuts us off from interpretive possibilities, it also limits our being. If we can no longer "rise at will / In the infinite void," that is because we have been "bound down/ To earth by [our] narrowing perceptions." And so it goes the other way around as well, of course. If we can open "the doors of perception," we can gain access not only to new ways of reading the world but above all to new ways of being in the world, new modes of life.

One of the themes running through Blake's books, then, is the struggle that takes place between these different forces: between, on the one hand, those who would restrict and channel us into finite and inflexible forms of being "bound down / To earth by their narrowing perception," and, on the other hand, those who refuse that force or will, those who resist by seeking joy rather than accepting confinement into the "red round globe" of the limited self to which, as Oothoon puts it in *Visions of the Daughters*, "they" tell us we have to be restricted. And it precisely in this context that we can look back to the little chimney sweeper in *Songs of Experience* and recognize the wider significance of his defiance of authority, his insistence on dancing and singing rather than simply agreeing – like his counterpart in *Songs of Innocence* – to wear "the clothes of death."

We need to see, however, that what is at stake here is a relationship to modes of social power and authority more generally. Hence the significance of the reference to "God & his priest & king" in "Chimney Sweeper" of *Experience*. These larger social forces operate (and hence they can also be contested, questioned, resisted) at the level of the individual self. Or rather, to be more precise, the self can be thought of as a site contested by larger social forces either as they attempt to squeeze and restrict our energies and desires, or, alternatively, as they are beaten back and joy and desire are allowed to flourish.

Hence there is a seamlessness in the logic of authoritarianism traced by Blake's illuminated books. We move along the scale from the local and the individual – the individual self contending with the command "Thou shalt not" – to the collective and the social. We can see that there is a direct relationship between the logic of moral commandments at the individual level (that is, at the level of an individual encounter with a particular text or commandment) and the larger forces of the state and state power more generally.

Thus it should come as no surprise that moral commandments, including those of the Bible, were seen by Blake as "the basest & most oppressive of human codes," because, "being like all other codes given under pretence of divine command [they] were what Christ pronounced them, The Abomination that maketh desolate, i.e., State Religion, which is the source of all Cruelty."[9] By directing our individual actions and seeking to make us adhere to certain moral codes conveyed to us in the act of reading itself, particularly reading the Bible (exactly as proposed and encouraged at the time by evangelical activists and propagandists such as Hannah More), these moral codes serve as the very backbone of state religion, and hence of the power of the state. Or in other words, the state depends for the exercise of its power not simply on armies or police forces but above all on our regulation as morally instructed individuals.

The proliferation of institutions of power we see throughout Blake's works runs the gamut from the church "appalled" by the chimney sweeper's cry or the palace down whose walls the soldier's sigh turns into blood in "London," or the church in which the parents of the little chimney sweeper in *Songs of Experience* pray to "God & his priest & King," to the "castles and high spires" where "kings and priests may dwell" in *Visions of the Daughters*, and on to the "Churches: Hospitals: Castles: Palaces" which we see in *The Song of Los*, which, "like nets & gins & traps," are intended to "catch the joys of Eternity," closing and restraining "Till a Philosophy of Five Senses was complete," which Urizen, weeping, gives "into the hands of Newton & Locke."[10] Here again Blake explicitly links the formation of individuals as enclosed self-regulating units governed by the limits of the five senses to the larger processes of state power, and to oppression more generally.

This explains the importance in Blake's work of moral codes intended to regulate our behavior as individuals. Not only are moral commandments such as those of the Bible "the most oppressive of human codes," but the king himself is depicted in Blake's work – in flagrant violation, by the way, of the prevailing laws against blasphemy and seditious libel – as the "guardian of the secret codes."[11] But the point is that while we can see and hear the "mind-forged manacles" at work all around us, while we can (sometimes at least) take heed of the priests in black gowns walking their rounds and binding with briars our joys and desires, we are not always necessarily caught in their trap. The Bible with its "sacred codes" can be thought of as what Blake, echoing Tom Paine, refers to as a "state Trick," and, at that, one through which "the People at all times could see," even though they may not always have had "the power to throw [it] off."[12] Hence the continuous struggle between those armed with codes and those defying them; between regulation and desire; between the learned and the unlearned; between social, political, and religious institutions and the limitless energies, the infinite capacities, of those who refuse to be "bound down / To earth by their narrowing perceptions," those who would throw off or smash through the prison of the five senses, those who would reject the dictates and commandments of moral codes and, with them, of state religion and state power, of God and priest and king.

Jesus Christ plays a key role in Blake's depiction of this struggle between those in power and those trying to evade it. For if, by way of opposing the Moral Virtues and the endless project embodied in moral codes of "Domineering over others," Christ "supposes every Thing to be Evident to the Child & to the Poor & Unlearned," the point is not merely that he offers a different way of reading the world around us, but that he also offers a different mode of living and being in contestation of moral codes and other "tricks" of the state and the guardians of power. For he embodies and expresses the creative power that we mistakenly surrender, or are perhaps coerced into surrendering, insofar as we accept our reduction into limited and finite forms of being cut off from the infinite. Blake's Christ is in this sense the embodiment of the power of the human form divine, or in other words the generative and creative power of which humans are capable when they reject the notion of a transcendent God standing outside of them in a position of judgment and punishment.

Accepting that there is an external God who is outside and beyond us and who is therefore in a position to command us can be seen, from this point of view, as an endorsement of the logic of commandments and codes more generally. Seeking to escape the power of commandment almost inevitably involves seeing the generative and creative power often projected onto God as in fact a human attribute more appropriately put to creative social and aesthetic uses. Moral codes must be broken, in other words, because they are among the mechanisms binding us and cutting us off from the infinite generative and creative power of which we are capable (a question to which we will return in greater detail in the chapter devoted to Blake's understanding of the imagination).

This is a point to which Blake frequently returns in the treatment of power in his work. In one of the Memorable Fancies of *The Marriage of Heaven and Hell*, the narrator depicts an encounter with one of the guardian Angels, the protectors, of the established moral order, in which one of the rebellious Devils insists that "there is no other God" beyond the human. "The Angel hearing this became almost blue but mastering himself he grew yellow, & at last white pink & smiling," we read. He then replies, "Thou Idolater, is not God One? & is not he visible in Jesus Christ? and has not Jesus Christ given his sanction to the law of ten commandments and are not all other men fools, sinners, & nothings?" To which the Devil fires back the response, "If Jesus Christ is the greatest man, you ought to love him in the greatest degree; now hear how he has given his sanction to the law of ten commandments: did he not mock at the sabbath, and so mock the sabbaths God? murder those who were murderd because of him? turn away the law from the woman taken in adultery? steal the labor of others to support him? bear false witness when he omitted making a defence before Pilate? covet when he pray'd for his disciples, and when he bid them shake off the dust of their feet against such as refused to lodge them? I tell you," the Devil concludes, "no virtue can exist without breaking these ten commandments: Jesus was all virtue, and acted from impulse: not from rules."[13] To break the rules is in this sense to defy the logic of commandment and hence of established power.

Blake consistently shows the struggle to either squeeze our being into restricted and limited forms of selfhood or to resist and contest that reduction and limitation and to assert the contrary mode of joyous prolif-eration as the most important site for the contestation of power. The political vision at stake here would have separated Blake quite distinctly from many of the radicals of his day, for whom, as we have seen in other chapters, self-regulating individuality was the very key to political liberty. What Blake is suggesting in his work is not only that the self-regulating individual is, far from the basis on which to formulate a project for political liberation, a trap into which we fall at our peril. To embrace limited individuality as the basis for a program of political liberation is to condemn that program to failure from the very outset. On the contrary: the path to true liberation must begin with the demolition of the contours of the self.

One of the most powerful of Blake's depictions of such a demolition occurs in *America: A Prophecy*, the illuminated book that is often taken to mark Blake at his most expressly political. Although a long and influential line of scholarship has read Blake's *America* as a straightforward depiction of the American revolution and war of independence, the text takes us in a very different direction than that taken by the American revolutionaries. It uses precisely the mode of vision advocated by Blake to imagine a far greater political and indeed psychoaffective transformation than was ever countenanced by those revolutionaries or their ideological heirs among the radicals of 1790s London.

For what we see at the end of *America* is a vision of renewal of the "fiery joy"[14] that Urizen had "perverted to ten commands,"[15] or in other words a breaking out of the confines and limits of "the cavern'd man." This is depicted in Blake's text quite literally as "bursting the stony roof" of our limited existence, a smashing away of the "five gates" of the "law-built heaven," a fiery and explosive conjunction in which "their bolts and hinges melted / And the fierce flames burnt round the heavens, & round the abodes of men." It is in this conjunction that Orc, the very spirit of fiery rebellion, declares to Urizen, with reference to his commandments, "That stony law I stamp to dust: and scatter religion abroad / To the four winds as a torn book, & none shall gather the leaves."[16] This scene of revolutionary liberation is so important in understanding Blake because it insists that the struggle against power and against the forces of commandment and of the moral codes that would seek to confine us and strip us of our own generative and creative power takes place at the level, at the very horizon, of the individual self. If there is a "law-built heaven," in other words, it exists not simply at the level of castles and palaces and churches and other social institutions, but also in the forms of engineering and individualization to which those institutions devote themselves, that is, precisely in the processes of binding and restriction that would reduce us to a caverned and limited existence stripped of creative potential. "The stony law" operates and has power exactly in the enforcement of the limits of the self. What we need, then, is to burst forth out of and beyond those limits, to reach out to the fiery potential and joy of our limitless collective imagination – and an altogether different kind of power.

CHAPTER 6

Time

Ah Sun-flower! weary of time,
Who countest the steps of the Sun:
Seeking after that sweet golden clime
Where the travellers journey is done.

Where the Youth pined away with desire,
And the pale Virgin shrouded in snow:
Arise from their graves and aspire,
Where my Sun-flower wishes to go.

The eight deceptively simple lines of "Ah! Sun-Flower" in *Songs of Experience* engage one of the themes to which Blake turned most often in the illuminated books, namely, the question of time. Different notions of time are registered everywhere in Blake's work, in all kinds of ways, whether thematically, as in this case, or more subtly in terms of the relationship of rhyme or meter to temporal patterns, or in terms of a set of philosophical or theological reflections on alternative modes of temporality, or, finally, in terms of the temporal structure expressed by the open nature of Blake's texts themselves.

Several different forms of time are marked out in the sunflower poem, and we might think of it as a meditation on the relationship and interaction of these different temporal modes. We have first of all the notion of linear time: the time of a journey to which the poem refers, which follows an arc or a line from beginning through the middle to end. We have the notion of diurnal time whose progress is repeatedly marked by the sunflower, or in other words the time of cyclical repetition according to which each day repeats the pattern of the day before it. And we have the notion of life-time, which combines both other notions, depending on whether we think of a life-time as marking in effect a straight line from birth to the finality of death (assuming death is final of course) or as marking a cyclical pattern of repetition and rebirth.

Blake was interested in all these different modes of time, and particularly in the interactions or contradictions between them, or what happens when they collide with each other. We have seen in previous chapters how the grave, which in so many ways can so obviously be thought of as the site of death and finality, can also in Blake's work be thought of as the source of life. This is a question with which Blake toyed in several different ways. He did so in terms of the materiality of his work, in which graving (as in, "grave the sentence deep," a line we discussed at length in Chapter 2) can be thought of quite literally as the source or origin of all his books, which sprang from the lines he en-graved in copper. And he did so also at a more symbolic or representational level, including in the sun flower poem, in which youthful figures – the youth pined away with desire and the pale virgin shrouded in snow – find themselves preparing to emerge from the grave into a new life, aspiring (breathing as well as having aspirations) in that "sweet golden clime" where life and death meet and converge or collapse into one another.

For indeed in "Sun-flower" the grave marks the site both of life and of death, both of the beginning and of the end. Paradoxically, it is the site of ending from which we begin; a paradox captured in the fact that the figures in question are both youthful (new, beginning, fresh, recent) and yet also already dead: the pale virgin is wrapped in a death shroud, after all, and the youth has – or *has been* – pined away: that is, as many readers of Blake have pointed out, he is dead from pining and/or he is encased in a coffin made of pinewood: literally pined away. So rather than marking the site to which the aged and the dead are led or condemned, the grave is here inverted to become the site from which the youthful spring forth. By reversing what is often thought of as the cyclical sequence of youth and old age, such an inversion also involves turning the logic of linear time on its head: death can now be seen to *precede* life, rather than following it: it is from death that we are born, rather than the other way around (we are born and live until death). Indeed, this brings what ought to be very distinct patterns of time – the linear and the cyclical – into quite close alignment with one another, a moment of mutual rupture, breakdown, crisis.

Does this help us understand the sunflower itself, and its time-weariness? The time to which the sunflower is enslaved, the time of which it is so weary, is actually both linear and cyclical. Every day, it has to follow the arc of the sun as it moves across the sky, tracing, in effect, the linear time of the day from morning to noon and night. And yet as each day follows the one before it and precedes the one after it there is also a kind of cyclicality in play as well, forcing the sunflower to repeat the same work over and over again from one day to the next. In either case, the sunflower is stuck in the structures of time, a state of stagnation brilliantly captured by the monotonous alliteration of the line, "countest the steps of the sun." What the sunflower wishes for all the more naturally, then, is an end to time, or at least to this kind of time: a moment where the weary traveler's journey can well and truly be said to be done. Where the sunflower wishes to go is that place where time short circuits, warps, and breaks down beyond repair, where beginnings and endings fall into one another and converge. Only with the end of time understood as either a line or a circle can the sunflower be relieved of the necessity of work, spared the weariness of time.

Weariness of time – or at least of a certain mode or conception of time – is a recurring theme in Blake's work. So too, is exploring what Blake called "eternity" as an alternative to conventional modes of time, or what he calls in *Milton* and other late works "the sea of time and space,"[1] a kind of morass that traps our individuated selves in the finitude of existence as defined by the prison of the five senses. Indeed, the running opposition we see in Blake's work between the finite and the infinite is especially important in his treatment of time, where it hinges on the contrast between fixed or definite forms of time (days or hours as measured in clock time) as opposed to the eternal. "The hours of folly are measured by the clock," according to one of the proverbs of Hell in *The Marriage of Heaven and Hell*; "but of wisdom, no clock can measure."[2] To get at its fullest meaning, that line needs to be read alongside another of the proverbs: "Improvement makes strait roads, but the crooked roads without Improvement, are roads of Genius."[3] Folly against wisdom, improvement against genius: part of what is at stake in the contrasts Blake is making is the logic of progress and development that we associate with modernization, of which Blake, for his part, was an unrelenting critic.

Indeed, it is impossible to overstate the broader social and historical significance of Blake's contestation of the notion – really of different notions – of time, especially linear time or clock time. We have to remember that Blake was living and writing in an age when time had not yet settled down into the regular rhythms that today dominate our lives and subject us all to a minutely regimented grid of coordinated movements. Not just that, but he was writing in an age when the very notions of progressive linear time and its variants (clock time, national time, world time, or what we now call Coordinated Universal Time, tied to Greenwich Mean Time) were still very much subject to struggle and contestation.

At the level of individual lives and local communities in Britain, the shift in patterns of life from varying rhythms determined by natural or ecological cycles (diurnal time, the seasons, the harvest, etc.) to the steady monotonous tick-tock of industrial time took decades to unfold through the late eighteenth century and on into the nineteenth. Through the remorseless regime of bells and fines introduced by the likes of Josiah Wedgwood, workers in the newly developing industrial economy of Blake's day had to be relentlessly drilled – disciplined and punished – into accepting the tyranny of the clock and of clock-time as defining the structures and patterns of their everyday lives.[4]

Meanwhile, it took decades to destroy the localized sense of time in Britain, which tied each community to different and specifically local natural cycles (e.g., climate, sunrise, and sunset) determined by its geographical location, and to replace local time with the far more abstract logic of national time. Until the adoption of what was called railroad time, for instance, different railroads operated on widely varying local times (so Manchester-based companies used Manchester time, London-based ones used London time, and so on) and passengers had to sift their way through timetables set to different times, keeping their eyes on the multiple different clocks on station platforms. It wasn't until quite late in the nineteenth century (1880), long after Blake's death, that the long struggle to extirpate local time was concluded by the imposition on the country of an officially coordinated national time based on Greenwich Mean Time (GMT). And it took decades longer for GMT to be adopted or imposed elsewhere (Ireland operated on Dublin time until GMT was adopted in 1916, for example, which subordinated Ireland all the more closely to the tyranny of London).

In our day we may take clock time and universal time for granted, for better or for worse (no one thinks twice about the deep cultural and historical significance, for instance, of the temporal terms of reference in the conversation between the crew of a Qantas aircraft crossing the Pacific and air traffic controllers in Los Angeles about the arrival weather forecast: this information will be provided by Greenwich Mean Time; the forecast, that is, refers to the time of onset of clouds or winds not in terms of local Los Angeles time but in terms of London time, which has become the standard for universal time). But in Blake's day the struggle to impose clock time and national time on the country and the world was anything but straightforward. And it should come as no surprise that he should have been so vigilant, so attentive, as to its significance. As an independent artisan, a member of a dying class, the rhythms and patterns of his work and life were not – unlike those of a factory worker – subject to or determined by the tyranny of the clock. He started and stopped work when he needed or wanted or had to, not because it was a particular time of day (scholars are today perhaps among the last professionals whose patterns of work are, for better or worse, not strictly determined by either the clock or the calendar – indeed, I am writing these very sentences at just after ten o'clock on a beautiful sunny Saturday morning!). And yet Blake was keenly aware of the significance of the imposition of modern conceptions of time. The discourse of "improvement," that strategic phrase summoned by Blake in the proverbs of Hell, was not solely restricted to charting new roads, after all: it was also used to channel human energies according to the arbitrary needs of those in power; it was used to justify social destruction and upheaval, from the projects to "aerate" London by demolishing and opening up densely packed neighborhoods to the projects to "develop" and "civilize" Britain's colonial subjects in Ireland, India, and elsewhere – and for that matter Englishmen of the lower orders at home.

The discourse of "improvement" was also used to justify imposing new work practices on people, making them more efficient and productive, even if at the expense of their psychic and social well-being (a condition from which we suffer in an even more extreme form today). The proliferation of what Blake famously called "dark satanic mills" through England's "green and pleasant land," including the imposing burned-out hulk of the Albion Flour Mills which Blake would have seen every time he crossed Blackfriars Bridge to and from Lambeth, was one index of this.[5] It's vital to recognize here, however, that Blake's relationship to mills and the logic of industrial time was not only a matter of principle and external observation, but of experience as well. We return to this point in greater detail in the next chapter, but it's worth at least dwelling briefly here on the important fact that Blake's profession – copperplate engraving and printing – was taken to be the very model of the modern industrial assembly line because of the distribution of tasks through time that a then-modern printshop involved.[6] Work on such an assembly line had to proceed from one station and worker to another through all of the necessary steps in a logical, linear fashion – the more efficiently, the better and more profitably. The ideal of a printing workshop (which is why the earliest theoreticians of the modern assembly line seized upon it as exemplary of what they had in mind) was to use time-determined work discipline – passing the object of labor along from one worker to another through each stage of production – to efficiently produce a stream of faithfully identical copies of a single prototype.

Blake, as we know from our discussion of his printing practices in other chapters, was not merely uninterested in this kind of rational, efficiency-maximizing logic; he actively undermined, disrupted, and perverted it in his own method of printing the illuminated books. For, working alone and on his own time rather than as the master of a team of workers, he used the machinery and technologies of mass homogeneous production to produce, in the most inefficient way imaginable (though that in itself was probably not exactly his intention), a heterogeneous dribble of non-identical, highly differentiated "copies" of books for which no true "original" can be said to exist, insofar as each "copy" is also itself an "original."

As I have already noted, we will return to a fuller discussion of this in our treatment of Blake's understanding of the imagination in the next chapter. For now, however, I want to point out that there is an extremely important temporal component to Blake's method and the books produced as a result. And I want to argue that his critique of modern clock time, the time of "improvement," extended from the content of his works, so to speak – the kind of critique of time we see in "Sun-flower," for example – to their very form.

As we saw in previous chapters, the text of Blake's illuminated books can be said to exist – or really to be activated, realized, turned on, actualized – in the gap between the verbal and visual components of which the book is immanently constituted. As we read *The Marriage*, or *Urizen*, or one of the *Songs*, we move among and between words, images, and sounds, not only on any given plate, but also as we turn from one plate to another of the same book and beyond that in relation to other plates of other books, given the extent to which Blake explicitly ties the elements of his works to one another, and not only by recycling and repeating particular images and lines of text from work to work to work, across the commercial/artistic frontier of his own practice. Thus, as we have seen, Blake's works teach us to find meaning not just lying there inertly in the form of buried secrets waiting to be discovered, excavated, and interpreted according to a logic of "secret codes" or "sacred codes," which, as we saw in the previous chapters, was a logic that he reviled. Rather, they encourage us to *generate* meanings as we trace and retrace different interpretive paths among and between the verbal and visual components that *we* tie together in our ever-varying readings of his work.

Two related questions are at stake here then. One is the idea that the text does not exist as a static, lifeless, inert object to be read archaeologically; rather, it is brought to life in any number of unpredictable ways as it is read and re-read, even if only in terms of the unstable, unpredictable, dynamic relationship between words and images on any one plate of any one work. The other question, arguably more important for our task in the present chapter, is that the mode of reading we need to come to terms with Blake's texts is anything but linear. Rather, by their very nature, we read – we pretty much *have* to read – Blake's works backward and forward and sideways and in circles, never simply in a straight line. The freedom we are granted by Blake's work, in other words, is not only a freedom from the authoritarian logic of dictatorship, which would seek to impose on us a uniform code or guide to reading. It is also, and in a related way, a freedom from the pressures and contours of time itself – time as wearying and burdensome. Dictatorial or authoritarian texts also seek to impose a rigid time structure on us, in other words: we have to read them in a particular sequence in order for them to make any kind of sense at all. When you are confronted with a text like *The Marriage of Heaven and Hell* or the *Book of Urizen*, even if you *wanted* to you wouldn't really be able to say with any certainty where the beginning, middle and end are; or that there aren't in fact multiple and proliferating beginnings, middles and ends; or that they will stay in the same place even if you can tentatively identify each of them as such. Indeed, it's when you try to make them linear, when you try to read them like a novel – to force them into the stream of linear, progressive time – that you end up with the nonsense and gibberish that so many readers have unfortunately decided they have found in Blake's work. To release or activate the potential of Blake's books, you really do have to move in a different, and ever-changing, kind of sequence: to try to link one of the "Memorable Fancies" of *The Marriage* to another backward and sideways, and not just in a straight line; to link the line "Empire is no more!" from *The Marriage* to *America* to its recurrence in *Visions of the Daughters*, where that "same" line (or lines with which it is associated) is repeated; to consider the relationship of the young man emerging from the earth on plate 21 of *The Marriage* to the "same" young man emerging from the earth on plate 6 of *America* or plate 4 of *Jerusalem* or the top half of "Death's Door," one of the drawings Blake produced for an illustrated edition of Robert Blair's *The Grave*, to which we will return shortly.

The point that I am trying to make here is that, just as the imposition of linearity was essential to time and work-discipline, or, for that matter, certain reading practices associated with certain kinds of texts, the *lack* of linearity, indeed the resistance to linearity, is absolutely vital to the experience of reading Blake's works. The struggle to resist the logic of clock time and the time of "Improvement," in other words, is built into the way the works function, not only into the anti-industrial logic and method by which they were produced, and is certainly not limited to a representational critique of linear time and progress in the works themselves, including, among other places, in "Sun-flower."

This raises another point which is equally important to understanding the critique of linear industrial time we see everywhere in Blake's work. This has to do with the logic of repetition. In the proto-industrial logic so perfectly captured in the assembly-line flow of commercial engraving from which Blake sought to detach himself, repetition is the process that yields one identical print after another. Repetition, in other words, is the very key to homogeneity; it is the logic that produces a stream of identical interchangeable copies. In Blake's work, on the other hand, repetition produces difference rather than sameness; and the key here is that there are still various kinds of repetition taking place – repeatedly inking and printing the same plate, for example; repeating the same plate even if in different sequences; repeating certain lines and images. But these acts of repetition all also disrupt the very possibility of mere blind replication. Moreover, they do so in such a way that the linearity of time itself can be seen to involve the endless repetition of the same units over and over again: in other words, the industrial process and industrial, linear time, are really inseparable from one another, two sides of the same coin. Whereas repetition in Blake's work involves the generation and proliferation and flourishing of difference in tandem with a different, non-linear, non-cyclical form of time.

Let me offer a quick set of examples to illustrate this double point by reference to something I touched on briefly already but that is worth returning to in order to elaborate it a little further. Among the many lines and images that are repeated in Blake's work there is a particularly intriguing cluster of images: the clearest and most proliferating example of the larger theme I am discussing here. These images are brought together in Blake's drawing and white-line etching of "Death's Door," which, as I mentioned earlier, he produced for an illustrated edition of Blair's *Grave* (see Figure 6.1). They then separate into two separate but related streams: on the one hand, of the rising youthful figure from the top of "Death's Door," who, as I mentioned earlier, can be seen in different plates of *The Marriage* (Figure 6.2), *America* (Figure 6.3), and *Jerusalem*, among other sites; and on the other hand of the old man from the lower half of "Death's Door" (Figure 6.1), who appears in *America* (Figure 6.4), *The Gates of Paradise* (Figure 6.5), *London* (Figure 6.6) and other sites as well.

FIGURE 6.1. "Death's Door."

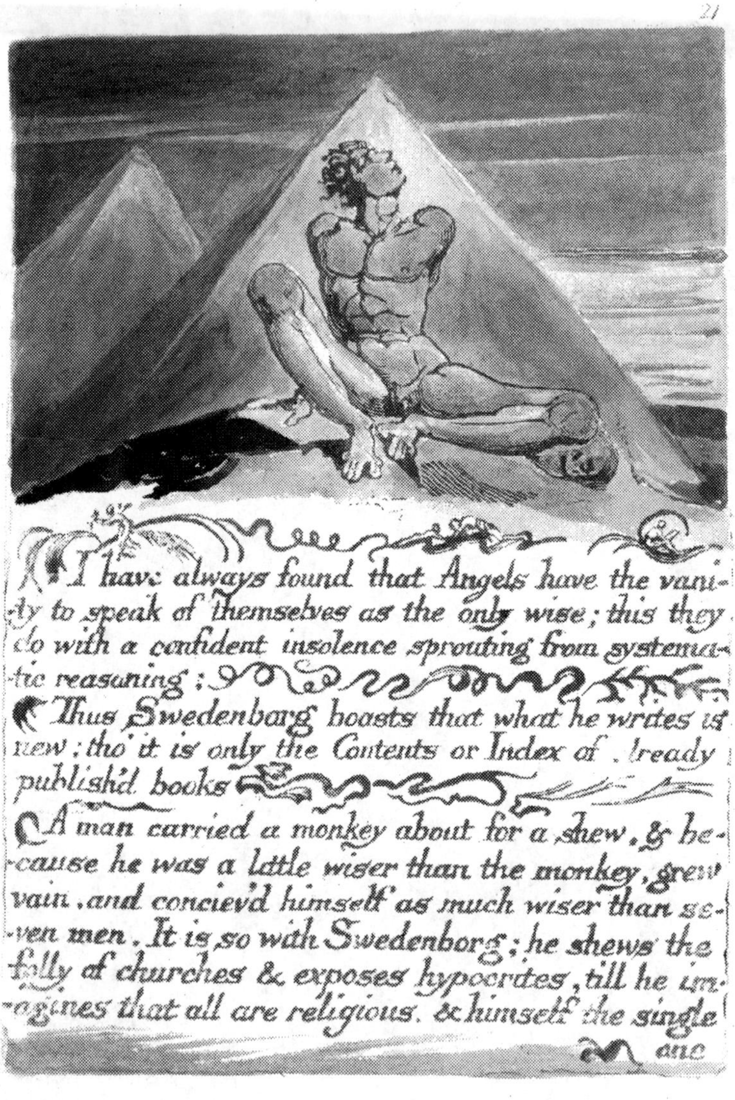

FIGURE 6.2.   Object 21 (Bentley 21, Erdman 21) of *The Marriage of Heaven and Hell*, copy D.

There are three parallel but related sets of points to make about this series of repetitions and its relationship to time in Blake.

The first involves the reiteration of a point I have already made: repetition in Blake's work involves producing change rather than

The morning comes, the night decays, the watchmen leave
    their stations;
The grave is burst, the spices shed, the linen wrapped up;
The bones of death, the cov'ring clay, the sinews shrunk & dry'd.
Reviving shake, inspiring move, breathing! awakening!
Spring like redeemed captives when their bonds & bars are burst;
Let the slave grinding at the mill, run out into the field:
Let him look up into the heavens & laugh in the bright air;
Let the inchained soul shut up in darkness and in sighing,
Whose face has never seen a smile in thirty weary years;
Rise and look out, his chains are loose, his dungeon doors are open.
And let his wife and children return from the opressors scourge;
They look behind at every step & believe it is a dream.
Singing. The Sun has left his blackness, & has found a fresher morning
And the fair Moon rejoices in the clear & cloudless night;
For Empire is no more, and now the Lion & Wolf shall cease.

FIGURE 6.3. Plate 8 of *America*, copy M.

replicating sameness. That is to say, what we might be tempted to refer to as the "same" image, in this case of the old man or the youth, is not exactly the "same" insofar as it appears in different contexts in each of its iterations. Moreover, the image itself intervenes in and alters the

FIGURE 6.4.   Plate 14 of *America*, copy M.

context in which it appears. So, whereas we might say of an assembly line
that the more products it produces through repetition, the more
sameness results, in this case, the more the "same" image is repeated,
the more change and difference is produced as a result.

FIGURE 6.5.   "Death's Door," from *For Children: The Gates of Paradise.*

The second point to make here again involves returning to and partially reiterating something I said a little earlier. When we encounter the youth or old man in these different contexts over and over again we almost inevitably find ourselves reading the relevant books in a way that disrupts

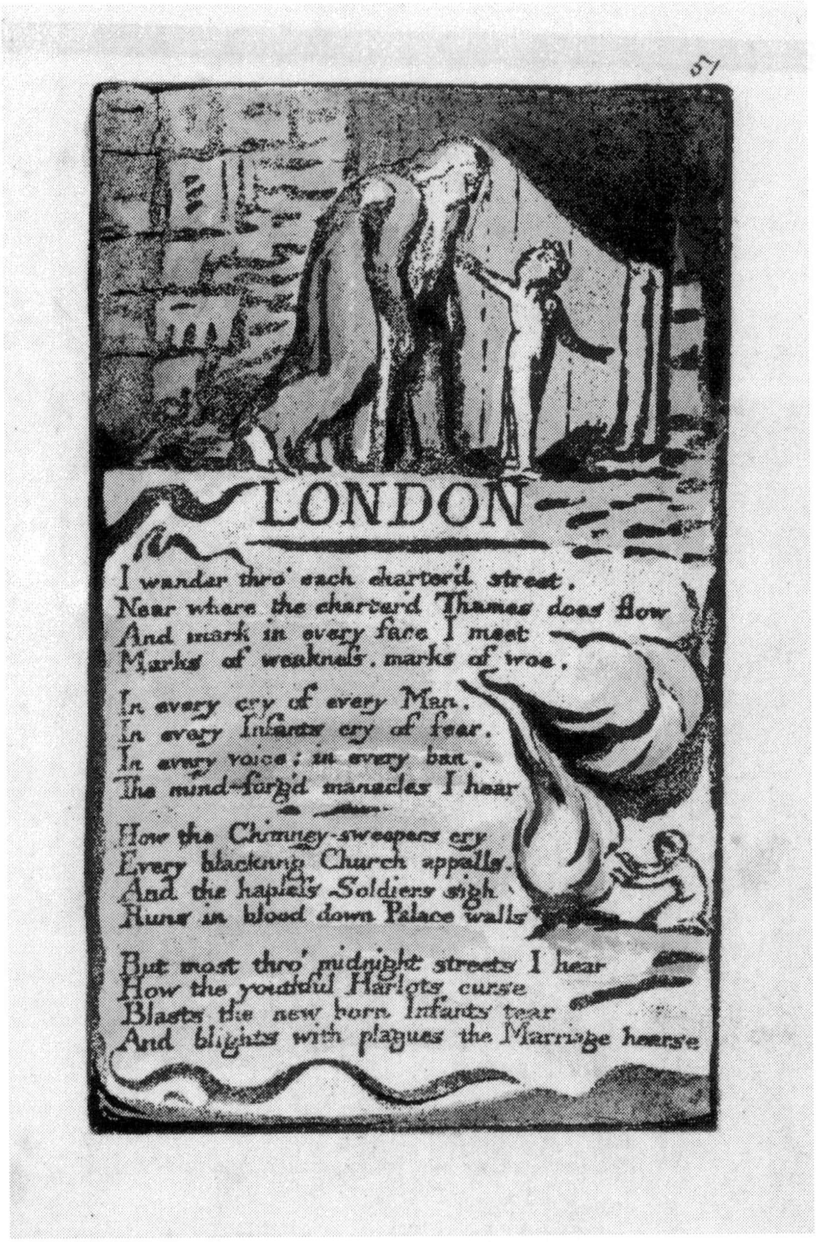

FIGURE 6.6. "London," from *Songs of Experience*, copy L.

and defies any straightforward or for that matter cyclical progression of time. When we see either figure in one context and then in another we are pushed to go back to where we first saw it. Such a movement involves many dynamics, but the one I want to point to in the context of the present chapter is that of time. Repetition in this case produces, far from a linear stream of time necessary to the logic of the assembly line, an experience of time that takes us backward and forward and sideways and diagonally between and among different texts, sites, moments.

This brings us to the third point I would like to register here, which makes this particular cluster of repeated images so important to our discussion of time in this chapter. If you go back and look at the image that unites the old man and youth (Figure 6.1), you will notice that it is, not coincidentally, called "Death's Door." The temptation offered by the image is to read the relationship of youth and old age in terms of death and life itself, and to see in that relationship a point of contact between a linear and a cyclical logic of time (that is, not coincidentally, the two forms of time treated also in terms of life and death in "Sun-flower"). Life can be thought of as a line leading from birth through youth, old age, and on to death. And, moreover, we can look at that line in two directions at once, either from the vantage point of youth heading toward old age, or from the vantage point of old age as the terminal point of youth, that point toward which youth inevitably leads. In addition, we can also read the juxtaposition of these different modes in terms of cyclical time, seeing life as a repeating (that notion again) cycle of birth, life, and death. That is, we can think of the two images as expressing the cyclical nature of time: the old man entering the grave at the end of life turns into the youthful figure rising from the grave to begin life all over again. As we saw in the discussion of the "Sun-flower" with which we opened this chapter, the grave itself can thus be thought of as both the endpoint and point of departure for life.

Now the reason all this is particularly pressing in terms of our discussion of time is that Blake, by alternately uniting and separating the figures of the old man and the youth in so many different contexts, is helping us think of the very constituent elements of time (linearity, cyclicality) as plastic: in alternately putting them together and separating them, we are either connecting or disconnecting the currents of time in ever-varying patterns. Sometimes we have life without death (the youth alone); sometimes death without the prospect of life or rebirth (the old man alone); and sometimes both together. Sometimes we come to one first and then the other, sometimes the other way around. This endless capacity for play pushes us to think of the extent to which there is no one way to think of time, in other words: it can go forward or backward or in circles depending on how *you* end up connecting these different images and strands of time to one another in your own reading, which itself can take you backward and forward and sideways and hence out of time understood as a straight line or an endless circle.

One discovery here, then, is that time itself is plastic and indeterminate: it is not fixed, inevitable, permanent, or given. It is endlessly repeated – but, as with all repetition in Blake's work, it is a repetition that also constantly changes, and indeed changes the more it is repeated. But there is an even more important discovery here as well: time gets activated and re-activated, turned on and turned off and around in a potentially infinite number of ways. This last point helps us think through Blake's conception of the eternal, and of the relationship in his work of time and eternity as expressed in one of the most profound of the proverbs of Hell in *The Marriage of Heaven and Hell*: "Eternity is in love with the productions of time."[7]

How indeed does eternity mesh with time? What the preceding discussion teaches us is that we can think of the notion of eternity in Blake as the source of limitless potential, or in fact simply as pure potential. From that source a potentially infinite number of lines or networks of connection through time (or between times) can be traced and retraced. Or, in other, words an infinite number of trajectories back and forth through time – constituting time in the process – can be launched from the infinite reservoir that is eternity.[8] Eternity contains all of the potential of those different temporal trajectories within itself in un-actualized, un-realized form. Eternity can thus be thought of as the source of time, to which time never extends.

This may all sound very abstract for now, but there are many different ways we can bring this discussion a little bit closer down to earth. For one thing, we have seen just this relationship of time and eternity in our discussion of how Blake's texts work. When I suggested earlier that the text of Blake's works exist not as inert forms but rather in their actualization as we trace interpretive paths among and between the verbal and visual elements of which each work consists, there is a temporal dynamic in play in such an understanding of textuality. When we activate the networks and circuits of time in tracing our ever-varying interpretive paths through Blake's work, we are actualizing and realizing what had until then been merely potential; that actualization can be thought of as a switching on of time in relation to the potentiality of what Blake called eternity.

There are other ways of thinking about this dynamic as well. When we think of the illuminated books not as bound and fixed and determinate texts but as the sites or occasions for a potentially infinite number of constantly changing re-printings involving variations in all the different elements we have touched on in other chapters (sequence, inking, coloring, etc.), we can also think of any one version of any of the books not as a faithfully blind copy of a prior original but rather as one particular actualization of that infinitely vast potential. This too, involves, in Blake's own terms, the relationship of time to eternity; for that vast potential exists not *in* time or *before* time, but outside of time altogether. This is actually a point that Blake himself made quite explicitly in one of his notebook entries:

> Reengravd Time after Time
> Ever in their Youthful prime
> My designs unchangd remain
> Time may rage but rage in vain
> For above Times troubled Fountains
> On the Great Atlantic Mountains
> In my Golden House on high
> There they Shine Eternally

Thus one can think of Blake's designs existing in an eternal space from which they can always be actualized in different ways by being repeated. So we return again, as it were, to our previous discussion of repetition to see all the more clearly the relationship of time and repetition to eternity in Blake. Time is generated by, it exists in, the endlessly proliferating repetitions of the infinitely vast potential contained in eternity. That is a potential, a richness, a variety that no clock or set of scales could ever measure.

CHAPTER 7

Making

Little lamb who made thee
Dost thou know who made thee
 – "The Lamb"
Did he smile his work to see?
Did he who made the Lamb make thee?
 – "The Tyger"

Two of Blake's best-known poems, "The Lamb" and "The Tyger," are about making, one of the central recurring themes in Blake's thought and work, along with joy and desire – notions from which it is inseparable. "Making," for Blake, marks the convergence of our joys and desires with our imaginations; it is the truest and fullest form of imaginative practice. And hence, as I hope to show in this chapter, making might even be said to constitute for Blake the very essence of our being.

The relationship of making and being is precisely the connection explored by these two well-known plates, the one from *Songs of Innocence*, the other from *Songs of Experience*. "The Lamb" unfolds as a series of questions in the first stanza, framed by the pair of lines "Little lamb who made thee / Dost thou know who made thee." A series of half-answers ("Little lamb I'll tell thee") follows in the second stanza: "He is called by thy name / For he calls himself a Lamb: / He is meek & he is mild, / He became a little child: / I a child & thou a lamb, / We are called by his name." I say half-answers because these lines provide a framework of blanks waiting to be filled in rather than definite answers as such. The immediate temptation, of course, is to read Jesus Christ into the open blanks, but, even having done so, we need to be wary not to think of the reference in conventional theological terms. Here, "I" and "thou" and "we" and "he" all converge into one another.

One way to think about this is to imagine, of course, the convergence of being that – according to the strands of antinomian thought we have discussed in previous chapters – links all of us to each other and to our common participation in God. Many consequences follow from such a reading. Most significant perhaps is the ever-tighter convergence of meaning between making and being. Making is not a static affair, done once and for all; to make and be made is to be an ongoing part of this convergence of I-you-we-he. Thus, in that sense, the fully commensurate answer to the question "who made you" really is, quite simply, just as the second stanza puts it, "you are part of something greater than yourself." Being and making are directly aligned with one another: two sides of the same coin. To make and to be made, at least under certain circumstances, is to participate in this common form of being which Blake called God; and to participate in this common form of being is also to make, to create, to produce. This yields another important consequence of this reading of the text. For another way of thinking about this convergence of being and making is to turn the relationship the other way around: insofar as you are part of something greater than yourself, you participate in that common being in the very act of your own creation. In the act and process of making, you are yourself – but you are also God.

That may sound a bit over the top, and indeed perhaps it is: we are talking here about a form of religious faith, after all, and not merely abstract philosophical speculation. But let's bear it in mind as one possible interpretive outcome. And with that in mind let's turn to "The Tyger," a text that has been read countless times in terms of the mystery of creation in all kinds of cosmic, religious, and theological ways. I don't intend to dispute those readings, but I would like to ground them a little further in Blake's specific thinking through of the double question of making and being.

"The Tyger" in a sense raises the stakes of the questions posed in "The Lamb." A similar set of questions to the ones posed in the first stanza of the earlier poem drives much of the energy of the later one. Now, however, the question isn't exactly "who made you?" but rather, in effect, "who could *possibly* have made you?" Or, in other words, "what kind of unfathomable and all but unimaginable power went into your creation, made your creation possible?" Here in other words the fact of creation is nothing short of miraculous, not because of the created object but rather because of the status of the creator: we recognize the divine power of creation precisely because such an act could only ever involve divine, miraculous power. This pushes us away from contemplating the object of creation to thinking about the creator. "What immortal hand or eye / Could frame thy fearful symmetry?" And indeed, in the poem's closing lines, "What immortal hand or eye / *Dare* frame thy fearful symmetry?" Or in other words, "who could *possibly* possess the unfathomable and unimaginable power that went into your creation?"

The plate itself provides, perhaps, some of the answers to these latter questions (see Figure 7.1). The first thing we notice about the plate is that, for all the famously repeated references to "fearful symmetry," the tiger itself is anything but symmetrical. Given the way Blake has drawn the animal with separated legs and paws, it could never be symmetrical. And in the various copies of the plate the tiger goes from looking awkward to looking disoriented, silly, or churlish, all of which undermine what one would have thought was the divine and/or cosmic nature of the plate. As the merest glance through his work demonstrates, Blake knew perfectly well how to draw human, divine, natural, or supernatural figures of fear, terror, and awe. He just didn't do it for this totally uninspiring – and asymmetrical – tiger.

In fact the plate's only vaguely symmetrical characteristic is the neat division of the six-stanza poem into two three-stanza sections separated by the line that, more or less (but not quite) halfway up, runs horizontally across the plate, connecting that offshoot of grass on the bottom left to the tree on the right and the title at the top. But because it splits off into those three different and discontinuous directions, that connection in itself disrupts its own partial symmetry; or, rather, it draws attention back to the words and away from the asymmetrical visual frame containing them.

Several consequences follow from these observations. One is that the plate seems to deliberately undermine the cosmic or mysterious status of the tiger as contemplated object. Another is that the plate's asymmetrical frame paradoxically emphasizes the symmetrical balance of the words rather than the images. Those two combined help pull the emphasis away from symmetry in a visual sense to other forms of symmetry; and hence they help pull our attention away from the tiger and, more and more, toward "The Tyger," that is, the plate, and in particular the poem itself. Once again we are reminded that what is at stake here is not the cosmic mystery of the creation as an object but rather the act or process of creation and the unfathomable power of the creator.

And suddenly things seem much clearer; our reading snaps into place (even if, as always, it is far from the only reading of this text). "Did he smile his work to see? / Did he who made the Lamb make thee?" Of course he did: the maker is Blake himself. He made "The Lamb" and he made "The Tyger," and there can be no doubt whatsoever that Blake smiled as he peeled first the one and then (five years later) the other out of the bed of his rolling press, seeing each of his inky creations for the first

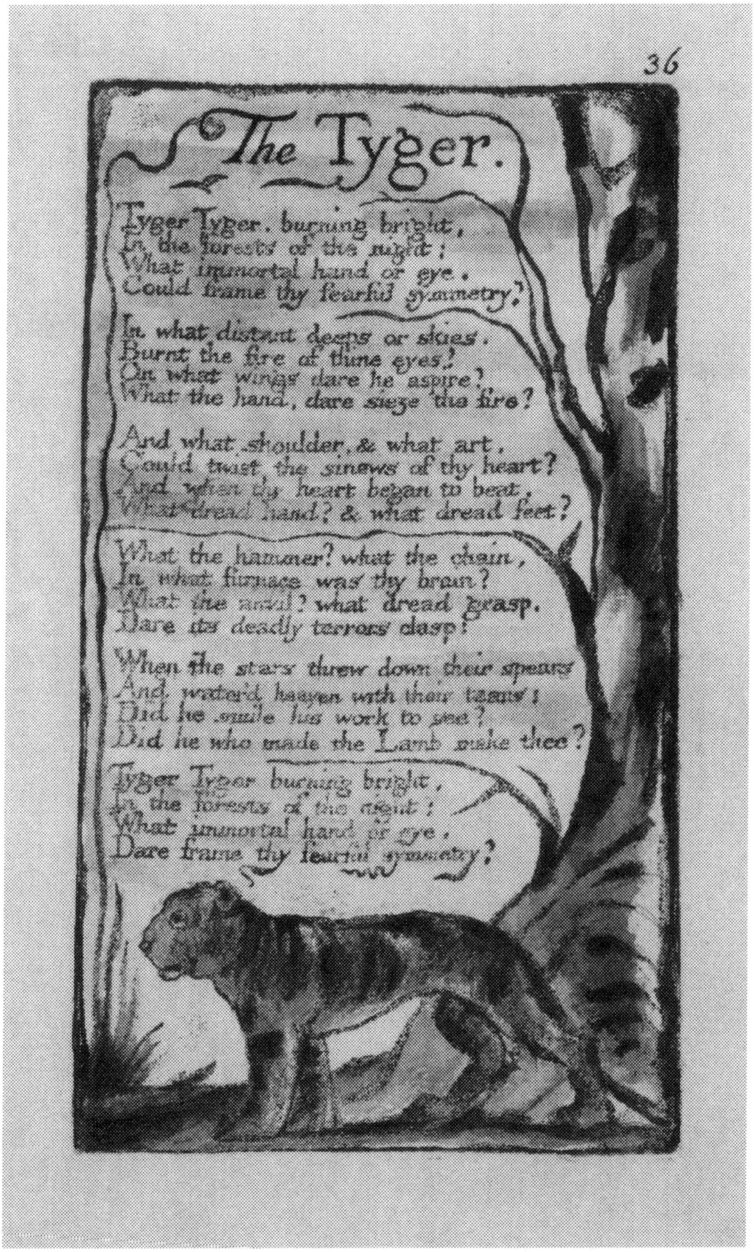

FIGURE 7.1. "The Tyger," from *Songs of Experience*, copy L.

time. All kinds of new forms of symmetry – and they are much more perfectly symmetrical than anything on the printed plate – now come rushing to our minds. There is the harmonious symmetry of the copper plate and the page printed from it, which would have been revealed for the first time exactly at the moment when Blake carefully peeled off the paper from the inked copper plate in the bed of his press (see Figure 7.2). There is the symmetry of positive and negative images, the former on the paper, the latter on the plate (see Figure 7.3). There is the matching symmetry of the mirrored words facing each other, the ones on the paper being the exact inverse of the ones on the copper – and now properly legible for the first time only because of that symmetry and the miracle worked by the rolling press. The words are thus symmetrical both in the sense that the parts of the poem balance each other within the frame posed by the opening and closing stanzas ("Tyger, Tyger burning bright . . .") and in the sense that in printed form they represent the perfect symmetry of Blake's art of printing.

Such a reading confirms all the more our suspicion that this is a text about Blake as artist, and the creative process of art itself. Far from

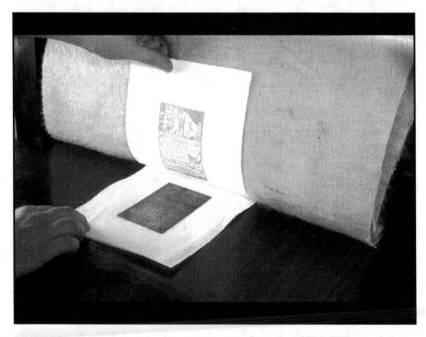

FIGURE 7.2.   From a printmaking session using facsimiles of Blake's copper plates.

FIGURE 7.3.   From a printmaking session using facsimiles of Blake's copper plates.

displacing the cosmic and theological language of the plate, though, it appropriates their energies. The act of imagination and of artistic creation expresses the divine; more than being a divine act, it is, in fact, what our very divinity as human beings consists of. This is a point that Blake made frequently over the years. "God only acts & Is, in existing beings or Men," he insists.[1] But it's not just that we exist together in God; our common existence in God is expressed in acts of imagination and of artistic creation. "The Eternal Body of Man is THE IMAGINATION," Blake writes; "that is God himself," the "Divine Body" of which "we are his Members."[2] It manifests itself, he adds, "in his works of art." Hence, as he puts it, "the whole Business of Man Is The Arts & All Things Common."[3] For Blake, as Northrop Frye once brilliantly argued this point, "we do not perceive God." Rather, he writes, "We perceive *as* God."[4]

There is more at stake here, however, than even Frye's argument allows. For in expressing our imagination through art or in other words through the act of artistic creation, we are expressing our common existence in God. Art, indeed, ceases to be either an elite practice or a mere commercial domain for buying and selling of the crudest variety (which it has certainly become in our own day); it becomes a common endeavor of all things and all people. And that too – humanity precisely in its common existence – expresses the divine and creative power of God.

The reason that this point is so vitally important to understanding Blake is that it captures and occupies the exact center of so many of the questions through which we have been working our way in this book: first, the common shared divinity of humankind; second, the enormous significance of joy and desire as the forces that take us beyond the limits of the self-regulating bourgeois individual confined, buried, restricted to the five senses, connecting us instead to our common shared being in God; and, finally and most clearly, the role of the imagination as the force that expresses our common divinity (common in all senses of that term). We are reminded here, however, of some of the other questions that have come up in this book. For one thing, our access to this common existence, and to the infinite capacities with which it is bound up, is anything but to be taken for granted. There is a struggle between the power of joy and desire and, on the other hand, those malevolent social forces that would seek to limit and confine us into units of being "barr'd and petrify'd against the infinite," cutting us off from our own capacities and our own potential. Thus it is no coincidence that art and the imagination, in Blake's work, become the central stage in the struggle over our very existence, our modes of life and of being. As we strive to maintain and express our creative and imaginative energies and capacities, there are those forces that aim to capture them and to contain and to smother our very existence.

This explains the sense of urgency attending some of Blake's comments about the status and significance of art and the imagination as the expressions of our creative human energies. "Without unceasing Practise nothing can be done," Blake writes. "Practice is Art," he adds. "If you leave off you are lost."[5] This reinforces the convergence of making and being that we discussed earlier with reference to "The Lamb" and "The Tyger." Our own existence is bound up with our imaginative and creative efforts; art as such is in this sense only one manifestation of our more general predisposition, our striving, to sustain our being through imaginative and creative practice, without which we are, for Blake, truly lost in that we abandon or are stripped of a certain degree of our own being.

We can express this differently by saying that for Blake, art, imagination, and making are essential to life, or at least the life of the dynamic, energetic, joyous forms of being in which he is interested. Our imaginative capacities are thus extensions of our very being. "This world is a world of imagination and vision," Blake once wrote to a critic who accused him of losing track of the distinction between imagination and reality. "I see every thing I paint in this world, but every body does not see alike," Blake insists; "as a man is so he sees." He adds, "You certainly mistake when you say that the Visions of Fancy are not to be found in This World. To me This World is all One continued Vision of Fancy & Imagination & I feel flatterd when I am told so."[6] Or in other words we constitute the world and reality itself through the exercise of our imaginative capacities. Reality is not simply handed to us as given by some other force or power; it is generated, directed, and determined by the agency of human intervention.

The point here is not simply that art as practice is far more important for Blake than art for art's sake. It is that there is no meaningful distinction between the forms of imaginative practice that go into making art as opposed to the forms of imaginative practice that go into shaping and making ourselves and the world around us. This dynamic is perhaps best expressed in one of the Memorable Fancies of *The Marriage of Heaven and Hell*, a scene in which the narrator is in effect kidnapped by one of the guardian angels of the established order and subjected to his power specifically in the sense of being subjected to his (the angel's) vision and conception of the universe. The angel thus projects a terrifying and dizzying vision of the universe intended precisely to cow the narrator into submission by attempting to strip him of his own imaginative capacities and to pin him down. The terrifying vision lasts as long as the angel maintains it, but upon his withdrawal from the scene the vision collapses – and not just the vision, but the world, the very reality, sustained by it, which is a reality intended to quell the ambitions of those who might otherwise seek to question it. Once the angel is gone, not just a new vision but an altogether new reality is revealed. "I remain'd alone, & then this appearance [that had been projected by the angel] was no more," says the narrator, "but I found myself sitting on a pleasant bank beside a river by moon light hearing a harper who sung to the harp. & his theme was, The man who never alters his opinions is like standing water & breeds reptiles of the mind."[7] It's not just reptiles of the mind that are at stake here, however. The point of this scene of shifting landscapes and realities is that there is no such thing as a stable, predetermined, given, and fixed reality. Realities are generated and sustained, imposed on one another, by the intervention of various forces, by a struggle over imaginative capacities. To go back to that letter from which I quoted a little earlier: the extension of Blake's claim that "as a man is so he sees," is that, as a man sees, so he is.

We have seen many variations on this theme in the discussion through this and the other chapters of this book. The significance of this restatement of the problem, however, is that it draws our attention to the sense that reality itself – not merely our own forms of being – is constituted and reconstituted through the struggle to either contain or diminish our imaginative capacities: to trap us into finite and limited forms of being "bound down/ To earth by their narrowing perceptions" and unable to "rise at will / In the infinite void," or, on the contrary, to unleash our imaginative potential and allow our desires to flourish.

Let me make this point more precisely: for Blake, there is a correspondence – a kind of fearful symmetry – between ourselves and the reality we inhabit. To be bound and limited to finite units of being who can access the world only through the confines defined by the "cavern'd being" imposed by the five senses is to see and experience a particularly limited and stunted form of reality. For to lose – or be stripped of – our imaginative and creative capacities is to be cut off from "the infinite," or in other words the potential to participate in the creation of ourselves in that expansive sense important to Blake, that is, through a flourishing of desire. In a related way it is also to be cut off from our capacity to shape and make the world around us, the very reality we inhabit. The limited existence of the five senses is not only finite; it lacks generative capacity; it has no choice but to accept the world as given. It is, in short, to be "lost," as Blake puts it in the *Laocoön*. Whereas, on the other hand, to maintain our imaginative capacities is to participate in those common energies and forces whose importance Blake identifies, and hence in the divine power of creation, both of ourselves (in collective terms) and of the world around us, the reality we inhabit.

This is why Blake places such emphasis on the need to resist the attempt by certain malevolent powers to strip us of our creative and imaginative abilities, powers that want, by compressing and regulating the very structures of our being, to control the world around us. Hence too the specific nature of the struggle to shape reality and to shape our forms of being, which, as I have suggested, amounts to a struggle over the exercise of our imaginative and creative capacities.

We catch the merest glimpse of this struggle in the passage from *The Marriage of Heaven and Hell* from which I quoted a little earlier, but it is one of the overriding themes of Blake's illuminated books. One of the recurring episodes recounted in different ways in the *Book of Urizen*, the *Book of Ahania* and the *Book of Los*, for example, is the complex process of transforming previously or potentially limitless bodies and energies into "branchy forms." This process of "organizing the Human into finite inflexible organs" necessarily cuts the human off from the infinite, thereby breaking the continuity between imaginative capacity and the reality we inhabit.[8] Even though he is the one who initiates and wants to have control over this process, Urizen himself is subject to such organization. Los rushes to "imbody" him, by "inclosing" his "fountain of thought."[9] This is language unmistakably reminiscent of Oothoon's lament in *Visions of the Daughters* that "They told me that I had five senses to inclose me up. / And they inclos'd my infinite brain into a narrow circle, / And sunk my heart into the Abyss, a red round globe hot burning / Till all from life I was obliterated and erased."[10] Once Urizen too, is "inclosed," he is cut off from "All the myriads of Eternity: / All the wisdom & joy of life," which "Roll like a sea around him, / Except what his little orbs / Of sight by degrees unfold." Thus, "his eternal life / Like a dream was obliterated."[11]

Now, admittedly, much of this undoubtedly sounds a little crazy. This is especially true of the bits where we see body parts "screaming" and "fluttering" as "some combin'd into muscles & glands / Some organs for craving and lust."[12] But we need to see Blake here using a figurative language to think through broader philosophical and religious, as well as social and political, matters. What he is interested in is not simply the relationship of being and making but specifically the extent to which they are either bound or unlimited. That is, to translate this into social terms, he was interested in the limits on creativity and the relationship of those limits to our very mode of being and the reality we inhabit. He was interested in the question of what happens to us when our creative capacities are stifled and channeled, or what happens when our bodily existence is so stunted and limited and cut off from the infinite that we lose any sense of agency or control of the world around us. And what happens when we are stripped of imaginative and intellectual capacities, reduced to mere bodies without minds, automata to be assigned a task and directed from on high.

For all the strangeness of the particular kind of language Blake used to think through these questions, though, he was hardly alone in asking them in the first place. He was more adamant than most about the dramatic loss of creative potential and agency with which he thought we were threatened. But perhaps that is because he happened to occupy an oddly privileged location from which to assess these developments, for reproductive engraving, the profession to which he was bound from his apprenticeship, was taken by key observers at the time to be the ideal form – the prototype as it were – for the modern factory and the modern assembly line.

Engravers were of course highly skilled, but on a modern assembly line workers were gradually de-skilled, and set to work in a series, with each worker attending to one particular task from the chain or sequence of tasks necessary to the production of the commodity at hand (hence mimicking the distribution of tasks from preparing the plate to inking it and on to pulling the prints in a print workshop like the one in which Blake would have worked as an apprentice). More important, however, workers on a modern assembly line were set to work under the direction of a supervisory power standing outside and (figuratively at least but also at times literally) above them. Each particular worker knew only the immediate task with which he or she was charged, not necessarily how it fits in the overall sequence, much less what the final product will look like or be. And thus the taskworker was stripped of creativity, ingenuity, direction, agency, even thought, and reduced to a mere mindless body carrying out the same repetitive task over and over again (a reality captured so perfectly in Charlie Chaplin's film *Modern Times*).

This chain of human bodies, each evacuated of creative, imaginative, or intellectual energies, could readily be seen as a machine or organism whose arms and limbs are individual human beings. And indeed these were precisely the terms used to describe the assembly line by observers like Andrew Ure and Charles Babbage in the nineteenth century and their predecessors in the eighteenth. A factory does best "where the mind is least consulted," as Adam Ferguson had pointed out in the 1760s; "where the workshop may, without any great effort of imagination, be considered an engine, the parts of which are men."[13]

What was at stake in the comparison of engraving to the modern factory, however, was not simply the distribution of tasks along an assembly line constituted by human beings stripped of their intellectual and imaginative capacities (if not altogether robbed of their very humanity), but rather the emphasis placed in commercial reproductive engraving – an emphasis that would find its perfection in the modern assembly line – on the separation of conception from execution. Engravers, we must remember, were not considered artists in the eighteenth or nineteenth centuries. (Indeed, engraving would not rise to the status of "art" until the twentieth century, when it had long ceased to play a role in the reproduction and dissemination of images on a commercial scale, having been overtaken by more efficient and less labor-intensive technologies such as lithography and photography, just as the printing of words had similarly shifted from laborious typesetting to printing on mechanized rotary presses). Designing an image was not considered the task of an engraver but of the artist whose work it was the engraver's job to faithfully copy by translating it, as it were, into a reproducible medium. The role of the engraver was thus limited to merely carrying out the repetitive task of executing, carrying out, the reproduction of someone else's original artistic conception (image, picture, portrait, etc.).

This separation of conception from execution was also integrally tied to, inseparable from, the all-important distinction between original and copy. The task of the engraver was not to produce an original work of art, but rather to produce a stream of copies of an original image or artwork. These copies might accrue a certain amount of commercial value, of course, but they were never comparable in status or value to the original non-reproducible work of art. Hence the social degradation of the engraver vis-à-vis the true artist was the flip side of the social degradation of the engraving seen as copy rather than true art. For the purposes of our discussion here, what matters is that for the theoreticians of the modern assembly line, especially Charles Babbage, the related distinction which they saw as key to the engraving trade, between conception and execution, on the one hand, and original and copy, on the other, helped explain and conceptualize the function of the modern assembly line. The idea of the assembly line, they argued, was to separate conception and, with it, any sense of imaginative or intellectual capacity, from the series of workers executing the repetitive task of production, who were stripped of intellectual agency. Similarly, the modern assembly line is premised on the distinction between an original (the prototype) and faithfully reproduced copies of that original (the actual commodities coming off the line).

For Blake, however, all these forms of distinction were anathema. He broke with the social, economic, and aesthetic universe of conventional reproductive engraving in several important ways – all of them essential for understanding the meaning and significance of his work. First, rather than accepting the premise of separation between the printing of words (which was an entirely different trade involving a separate division of labor completely distinct from that of the engraving business) and the printing of images (the domain of engraving as such), he aimed to unify both words and images in his work. Second, he utterly rejected the distinction between conception and execution. Not only did he unite the roles of poet and artist but he also broke down the distinction between the original conception of the work and its material printing and production. It was Blake himself who drafted the poems, sketched preliminary designs, and staged his work from ink or graphite on paper to wax, etching needles, acid, and copper, and on to inking, printing, coloring, sequencing plates, and binding them together.

There are several major consequences from all of this. As mentioned earlier, there is no distinction in Blake's work between conception and execution not only because he was responsible for and materially involved in both, but also because at no stage of his printing process is it possible to differentiate conception from execution. He composed and made changes to both words and designs through the entire process, and not merely in the "prototype" stage of paper drafts. As we have seen in previous chapters, he continued to make substantive changes, simultaneously conceptual and material, all the way through each successive stage, from inking and coloring to sequencing and binding. It is precisely as a result of this collapse of the categories of conception and execution in Blake's work that the distinction between original and copy also breaks down. There are no "originals" of any of the illuminated books, no prototypes (not even the copper plates themselves); there are only "copies," though they are anything but copies in the industrial sense of that term – that is, as opposed to an antecedent "original."

From these observations several others follow, all of them of immense social, religious, political, and economic significance for our understanding of Blake. He saw his method of work and of art as completely at odds with the quasi- or proto-industrial art industry that began to dominate England during his lifetime, and its attendant forms of distinction between the figure of the Artist (with a capital "A") and mere hack workers, tradesmen, and copyists – the equivalents in the visual art world of the grub street writers whose parallel social fate was bemoaned by George Gissing, among others, much later in the nineteenth century. Blake recognized and furiously condemned the stripping away of workers' imaginative and intellectual powers, their reduction to mere bodily physicality, which was proving so essential to the commercial and industrial world he saw coming into being all around him. He reviled the idea of a commercial system that relies for its profits on stripping away skills and reducing labor to its lowest common denominator. "Commerce Cannot endure Individual Merit," he fumed; "its insatiable Maw must be fed by What all can do Equally well at least so it is in England as I have found to my Cost these Forty Years."[14]

It would be a mistake, however, to assume that personal outrage and hurt drove Blake's thinking on these matters. From very early in his career, when he was still relatively prosperous, we can see the centrality of his critique of industrial and commercial logic to his work, beginning, as I have already noted, with the way in which his own mode of production turned the logic of the industrial revolution and its labor-saving technologies on its head. The insistence on the creative capacity of the imagination tied to joy and desire is, as we have seen, one of the themes running right through his work. The attempt to strip people of creativity and reduce them to limited forms of being is one of the overriding concerns of the illuminated books, and we see it at work everywhere from *Songs* and the *Marriage* to *Visions of the Daughters*, *The Book of Urizen* and on to *Milton* and *Jerusalem*.

More to the point, there is in Blake's critique of his age a fusion of aesthetic questions with moral, religious, political, and economic ones. Urizen's power is based on our reduction to mere "portions of life," the consequences of which are simultaneously religious, political, and economic, for example. Those subject to his power are as denuded politically and religiously (subject to "One King, one God, one Law")[15] as they are economically. For we see Urizen also in the guise of "the great Work master,"[16] who in Blake's vision exercises despotic control over an industrial and commercial mode of productive organization in which "each took his station, & his course began with sorrow & care / In sevens & tens & fifties, hundreds, thousands, numberd all / According to their various powers. Subordinate to Urizen."[17] Indeed, Urizen's status as "work master" is quite inseparable from his self-proclaimed divine power ("Am I not God said Urizen. Who is Equal to me").[18] After revealing himself as "A God & not a Man a Conqueror in triumphant glory,"[19] Urizen unfolds his true power: "First Trades & Commerce ships & armed vessels he builded laborious / To swim the deep & on the Land children are sold to trades / Of dire necessity still laboring day & night till all / Their life extinct they took the spectre form in dark despair."[20] For the purposes of our discussion here, what is most significant about Blake's treatment of Urizen is that the convergence of religious, political, and economic power is shown to be inseparable from the process of stripping away our imaginative capacities and reducing human life to all but dead bodily forms; bodies, that is, stripped of the creative power of the imagination.

What we see in Blake's work, then, is a convergence and common critique of several normally different and distinct forms of power, several different logics of command and authority: the religious form of power that separates an infinitely elevated creator over the debased creation (a relationship amplified by the conventional monotheistic view that people are but the degraded lesser copies of an original God); the economic form of power that elevates the unique position of command and authority over an army of workers stripped of intellectual agency and reduced to mere numbers; and the form of power that we have discussed extensively in other chapters of this book, which seeks to strip us of our imaginative capacities and reduce us to portions of life trapped in the prison of the five senses and thus barred and cut off from the infinite. These logics of power are all shown to be inseparable from one another in Blake's work.

For Blake, the imagination is vital to any effort to resist the encroachment of these forms of power; hence it appears as a site of struggle and contestation in his work. And, against the endeavor to restrict and contain our very humanity in portions of life cut off from the infinite – an endeavor we can understand simultaneously in political, religious, economic, and aesthetic terms – he insisted on the need to maintain our imaginative lives. This is to say that the imagination and making, the notion of the freedom to make, are the very keys to Blake's views of politics and religion and economics as much as his view of aesthetics. For Blake, as we have seen in the previous chapters, our being is defined by our desire: we exist not in definite or fixed forms created once and forever and then tediously and faithfully reprinted as though on a mass assembly line, but rather as ever-changing networks of relations articulated by our infinite desires. The essence of our being doesn't consist in a fixed set of properties and rights, but rather in our capacity to imagine, to desire, to make ourselves and the world around us. Thus Blake rejects the narrow, confined "knowledge" of confined individual selfhood, which his work allows us to recognize as the very basis of modern economic and political formations. And he affirms instead the joyous life of the prolific: life as an infinitely generative variety of re-makings, re-imaginations, re-becomings. This is a life of endless making; a life in which art and life itself are truly indistinguishable – art and life, that is, in the spirit of Blake.

Notes

Introduction

1 Letter to Dr. Trusler, August 1799 (Erdman, p. 703).
2 *Marriage of Heaven and Hell*, plate 19 (Erdman, p. 42).
3 Quoted in John Summerson, *John Nash: Architect to King George IV* (London: Allen & Unwin), p. 124. For more on the Regent Street project, especially in terms of speed and movement, see Richard Sennett, *Flesh and Stone: The Body and the City in Western Civilization* (New York: Norton, 1996), esp. pp. 325–29.
4 This is a question I discuss at length in my book *Making England Western: Occidentalism, Race, and Imperial Culture* (University of Chicago Press, 2014).

Chapter 1. Image

1 For an influential take on the relationship between entropy and aesthetics, see Rudolph Arnheim, *Entropy and Art: An Essay on Order and Disorder* (Berkeley: University of California Press, 1974).
2 Nelson Hilton, *Literal Imagination: Blake's Vision of Words* (Berkeley: University of California Press, 1983), p. 11.

Chapter 2. Text

1 Blake's annotations to Thornton (Erdman, p. 667).
2 Gerrard Winstanley, "A Watch-Word to the City of London," in *The Complete Works of Gerrard Winstanley*, ed. Thomas Corns et al. (Oxford University Press, 2009), vol. 2, p. 85.
3 "The Little Vagabond," in *Songs of Experience* (Erdman, p. 26).
4 *The Marriage of Heaven and Hell*, plate 6 (Erdman, p. 35).
5 See, for example, Blake's annotations to Watson's *Apology for the Bible* (Erdman, p. 618).
6 *The Marriage of Heaven and Hell*, plate 16 (Erdman, p. 40).
7 *The Marriage of Heaven and Hell*, plate 27 (Erdman, p. 45).

8 See Jacob Bauthumley, *The Light and Dark Sides of God*, in *A Collection of Ranter Writings from the Seventeenth Century*, ed. Nigel Smith (London: Junction Books, 1983), pp. 232–33.
9 "The Chimney Sweeper," *Songs of Experience* (Erdman, p. 23).
10 *The Marriage of Heaven and Hell*, plate 19 (Erdman, p. 42).
11 See *The Marriage of Heaven and Hell*, plates 17–20 (Erdman, pp. 41–42).
12 *The Everlasting Gospel* (Erdman, p. 524).
13 *The Book of Urizen*, plate 4 (Erdman, p. 72).
14 *The Book of Urizen*, plate 27 (Erdman, p. 83).
15 *The Book of Urizen*, plate 4 (Erdman, p. 72).
16 *The Book of Urizen*, plate 23 (Erdman, p. 81).

Chapter 3. Desire

1 "The Lamb," in *Songs of Innocence* (Erdman, pp. 8–9).
2 *The Marriage of Heaven and Hell*, plate 16 (Erdman, p. 40).
3 *The Marriage of Heaven and Hell*, plate 27 (Erdman, p. 45).
4 "The Divine Image" in *Songs of Innocence* (Erdman, pp. 12–13).
5 See Blake, *Songs of Innocence and of Experience*, ed. Robert Essick (San Marino: Huntington Library Press, 2008), pp. 10–11, 72–75.
6 *Book of Urizen*, plate 14 (Erdman, p. 77)
7 *Book of Urizen*, plate 5 (Erdman, p. 73).
8 *Book of Urizen*, plate 13 (Erdman, p. 77)
9 *Book of Urizen*, plates 27–28 (Erdman, p. 83).
10 *Book of Urizen*, plates 27–28 (Erdman, p. 83).
11 *There Is No Natural Religion* [b], plate 3 (Erdman, p. 2).
12 *Marriage of Heaven and Hell*, plate 14 (Erdman, p. 39).
13 *Europe*, plate iii (Erdman, p. 60); *Visions of the Daughters of Albion*, plate 3 (Erdman, p. 47).
14 *The Song of Los*, plate 4 (Erdman, p. 67).
15 *The Song of Los*, plate 4 (Erdman, p. 67).
16 "The Chimney Sweeper," in *Songs of Experience* (Erdman, p. 23).
17 *Europe*, plate 10 (Erdman, p. 63).
18 *There Is No Natural Religion* [b], plate 3 (Erdman, p. 2).
19 *There Is No Natural Religion* [b] (Erdman, p. 2).
20 *There Is No Natural Religion* [b] (Erdman, p. 2).
21 It's worth reading Ghassan Hage's *Against Paranoid Nationalism* for a succinct take on this question, staged via the work of the French theorist Pierre Bourdieu. See Ghassan Hage, *Against Paranoid Nationalism: Searching for Hope in a Shrinking Society* (Melbourne: Pluto Press, 2003).
22 *Laocoön* (Erdman, p. 273).

Chapter 4. Joy

1 *Laocoön* (Erdman, p. 273).

2 For more on Spinoza's distinction between substance and mode, see Spinoza, *The Ethics*, trans. Edwin Curley (London: Penguin, 2005); Warren Montag and Ted Stolze, eds., *The New Spinoza* (Minneapolis: University of Minnesota Press, 2008); Gilles Deleuze, *Spinoza: Practical Philosophy*, trans. Robert Hurley (San Francisco: City Lights, 1988).

3 See Henri Bergson, *Matter and Memory*, trans. Nancy Paul and W. Scott Palmer (New York: Zone, 1991), esp. chapter 3. Also see Michael Hardt, *Gilles Deleuze: An Apprenticeship in Philosophy* (Minneapolis: University of Minnesota Press, 1993) for an excellent discussion of Bergson.

4 *There Is No Natural Religion* [b] (Erdman, p. 2).

5 "Night," in *Songs of Innocence* (Erdman, p. 13).

6 "The School Boy," in *Songs of Experience* (Erdman, p. 31).

7 Samuel Coleridge, "Frost at Midnight," l. 52.

8 William Wordsworth, "Lines Written a Few Miles above Tintern Abbey . . . ," ll. 28–31.

9 *Jerusalem*, plate 34 (Erdman, p. 180).

10 *Marriage of Heaven and Hell*, plate 10 (Erdman, p. 38).

11 Annotations to Wordsworth (Erdman, p. 665).

12 *Marriage of Heaven and Hell*, plates 6–7 (Erdman, p. 35).

13 *Marriage of Heaven and Hell*, plates 6–7 (Erdman, p. 35).

14 *Visions of the Daughters of Albion*, plate 7 (Erdman, p. 50).

15 *Visions of the Daughters of Albion*, plate 3 (Erdman, p. 47).

16 *Visions of the Daughters of Albion*, plate 7 (Erdman, p. 50).

17 *Visions of the Daughters of Albion*, plate 7 (Erdman, p. 50).

18 *Visions of the Daughters of Albion*, plate 5 (Erdman, p. 49).

19 "London," in *Songs of Experience* (Erdman, p. 27).

20 *The Book of Urizen*, plate 4 (Erdman, p. 72).

21 *Visions of the Daughters of Albion*, plate 5 (Erdman, p. 48).

22 *America*, plate 8 (Erdman, p. 54).

23 *America*, plate 8 (Erdman, p. 54).

24 *America*, plate 8 (Erdman, p. 54).

Chapter 5. Power

1 *Jerusalem*, plate 22 (Erdman, p. 167).

2 Edmund Burke, *Reflections on the Revolution in France* (London: 1790), p. 49.

3 Annotations to Thornton (Erdman, p. 669).

4 Annotations to Thornton (Erdman, p. 669).

5 Annotations to Thornton (Erdman, p. 669).

6 Annotations to Thornton (Erdman, p. 667).

7 Annotations to Berkeley's *Siris* (Erdman, p. 664).

8 Annotations to Berkeley's *Siris* (Erdman, p. 664).

9 Annotations to Watson's *Apology for the Bible* (Erdman, p. 618).

10 *Song of Los*, plates 4 and 5 (Erdman, pp. 67–68).

11 *Europe*, plate 12 (Erdman, p. 64).

12 Annotations to Watson's *Apology for the Bible* (Erdman, p. 618).
13 *Marriage of Heaven and Hell*, plate 23 (Erdman, p. 443).
14 *America*, plate 8 (Erdman, p. 54).
15 *America*, plate 8 (Erdman, p. 54).
16 *America*, plate 8 (Erdman, p. 54).

Chapter 6. Time

1 *Milton*, plate 15 (Erdman, p. 110).
2 *Marriage of Heaven and Hell*, plate 7 (Erdman, p. 36).
3 *Marriage of Heaven and Hell*, plate 10 (Erdman, p. 38).
4 See E. P. Thompson, "Time, Work Discipline and Industrial Capitalism," in *Past and Present*, vol. 38, no. 1 (1967), 56–97.
5 *Milton*, plate 1 (Erdman, p. 95).
6 This is a point I discuss at great length in my book *William Blake and the Impossible History of the 1790s* (University of Chicago Press, 2003), pp. 78–154.
7 *Marriage of Heaven and Hell*, plate 7 (Erdman, p. 36).
8 As I have noted in other chapters, Henri Bergson's notion of the virtual and the actual can be very helpful in thinking through these questions in Blake.

Chapter 7. Making

1 *The Marriage of Heaven and Hell*, plate 16 (Erdman, p. 41).
2 *Laocoön* (Erdman, p. 273).
3 *Laocoön* (Erdman, p. 273).
4 Northrop Frye, *Fearful Symmetry: A Study of William Blake* (University of Toronto Press, 2004), p. 39. Emphasis in original.
5 *Laocoön* (Erdman, p. 274).
6 Letter to Dr. Trusler, August 1799 (Erdman, p. 702).
7 *Marriage of Heaven and Hell*, plate 18 (Erdman, pp. 41–42).
8 *Book of Los*, plate 4 (Erdman, p. 92).
9 Book of Urizen, plate 10 (Erdman, p. 75).
10 *Visions of the Daughters of Albion*, plate 3 (Erdman, p. 47).
11 *Book of Urizen*, plate 13 (Erdman, p. 77).
12 *Book of Ahania*, plate 4 (Erdman, p. 88).
13 Adam Ferguson, *An Essay on the History of Civil Society* (Dublin, 1767), p. 273.
14 "Chaucer's Canterbury Pilgrims" (Erdman, p. 573).
15 *Book of Urizen*, plate 4 (Erdman, p. 72).
16 *Four Zoas*, page 24 (Erdman, p. 314).
17 *Four Zoas*, page 33 (Erdman, p. 322).
18 *Four Zoas*, page 42 (Erdman, p. 328).
19 *Four Zoas*, page 95 (Erdman, p. 360).
20 *Four Zoas*, page 95 (Erdman, pp. 360–61).

Guide to further reading

EDITIONS AND CATALOGS OF BLAKE'S WORKS

G. E. Bentley Jr., ed., *Blake Books* (Oxford: Clarendon Press, 1977)

David Bindman, gen. ed., *Blake's Illuminated Books*, 6 volumes (Princeton University Press, 1991–95).

Martin Butlin, *Paintings and Drawings of William Blake* (New Haven: Yale Center for British Art, 1981).

David Erdman, ed., *The Complete Poetry and Prose of William Blake* (New York: Doubleday, 1988).

Robert Essick and Morton Paley, eds., *Robert Blair's The Grave, Illustrated by William Blake: A Study and Facsimile* (London: Scolar Press, 1982).

Robert Essick, ed., *The Separate Plates of William Blake: A Catalogue* (Princeton University Press, 1983).

Robert Essick, ed., *William Blake's Commercial Book Illustrations* (Oxford: Clarendon Press, 1991).

Robert Essick, ed., *Songs of Innocence and of Experience* (San Marino: Huntington Library, 2008).

Michael Phillips, ed., *The Marriage of Heaven and Hell* (Oxford: Bodleian Library, 2011).

Irene Tayler, ed., *Blake's Illustrations to the Poems of Gray* (Princeton University Press, 1971)

Biographies of Blake

Peter Ackroyd, *Blake* (New York: Knopf, 1996).

John Beer, *William Blake: A Literary Life* (Basingstoke: Palgrave, 2005).

G. E. Bentley Jr., ed., *Blake Records* (Oxford University Press, 1969).

 The Stranger from Paradise (New Haven: Yale Center for British Art, 2003).

Alexander Gilchrist, *The Life of William Blake* (1863; reprt. London: Dent, 1982).

Classic studies of Blake

Harold Bloom, *Blake's Apocalypse* (New York: Doubleday, 1963).

Jacob Bronowski, *Blake: A Man without a Mask* (London: Secker and Warburg, 1943).

David Erdman, *Blake, Prophet against Empire* (Princeton University Press, 1954).

Northrop Frye, *Fearful Symmetry: A Study of William Blake* (Boston: Beacon Press, 1965).

Robert Gleckner, *The Piper and the Bard* (Detroit: Wayne State University Press, 1959).

Geoffrey Keynes, *Blake Studies: Essays on His Life and Work* (Oxford: Clarendon Press, 1971).

A. L. Morton, *The Everlasting Gospel: A Study in the Sources of William Blake* (London: Lawrence and Wishart, 1970).

Kathleen Raine, *Blake and Tradition* (Princeton University Press, 1968).

Books on Blake, art, and printmaking

Morris Eaves, *The Counter-Arts Conspiracy: Art and Industry in the Age of Blake* (Ithaca: Cornell University Press, 1993).

    William Blake's Theory of Art (Princeton University Press, 1982).

Robert Essick, *William Blake, Printmaker* (Princeton University Press, 1980).

Michael Phillips, *The Creation of the Songs: From Manuscript to Illuminated Printing* (Princeton University Press, 2000).

Joseph Viscomi, *Blake and the Idea of the Book* (Princeton University Press, 1993).

General studies of Blake and Blake criticism

Mark Crosby et al., eds., *Re-Envisioning Blake* (Basingstoke: Palgrave, 2012).

Morris Eaves, ed., *The Cambridge Companion to William Blake* (Cambridge University Press, 2003).

Steven Goldsmith, *Blake's Agitation: Criticism and the Emotions* (Baltimore: Johns Hopkins University Press, 2013).

Nelson Hilton, *Literal Imagination: Blake's Vision of Words* (Berkeley: University of California Press, 1983)

Anne Mellor, *Blake's Human Form Divine* (Berkeley: University of California Press, 1974).

W. J. T. Mitchell, *Blake's Composite Art* (Princeton University Press, 1978).

Peter Otto, *Constructive Vision and Visionary Deconstruction* (Oxford: Clarendon Press, 1991).

Morton Paley, *Energy and the Imagination: A Study of the Development of Blake's Thought* (Oxford University Press, 1970).

Nicholas Williams, ed., *Advances in Blake Studies* (Basingstoke: Palgrave, 2007)

Social, historical, and political studies of Blake

Helen Bruder, *William Blake and the Daughters of Albion* (New York: St. Martin's Press, 1997).

Helen Bruder and Tristanne Connolly, eds., *Queer Blake* (Basingstoke: Palgrave, 2010).

Steve Clark and David Worrall, eds., *Historicizing Blake* (Basingstoke: Palgrave, 1994).

eds., *Blake, Nation and Empire* (Basingstoke: Palgrave, 2006).

Jackie Di Salvo, *War of Titans: Blake's Critique of Milton and the Politics of Religion* (University of Pittsburgh Press, 1983).

Jackie Di Salvo et al., eds., *Blake, Politics and History* (New York: Garland, 1998).

Michael Ferber, *The Social Vision of William Blake* (Princeton University Press, 1985).

Saree Makdisi, *William Blake and the Impossible History of the 1790s* (University of Chicago Press, 2003).

Jon Mee, *Dangerous Enthusiasm: William Blake and the Culture of Radicalism in the 1790s* (Oxford University Press, 1992).

Jon Mee and Sarah Haggarty, eds., *Blake and Conflict* (Basingstoke: Palgrave, 2009).

E. P. Thompson, *Witness against the Beast: William Blake and the Moral Law* (New York: New Press, 1995).

Nicholas Williams, *Ideology and Utopia in the Poetry of William Blake* (Cambridge University Press, 1998).

Index

Printed in the United States
By Bookmasters